Scottish mountain climbs

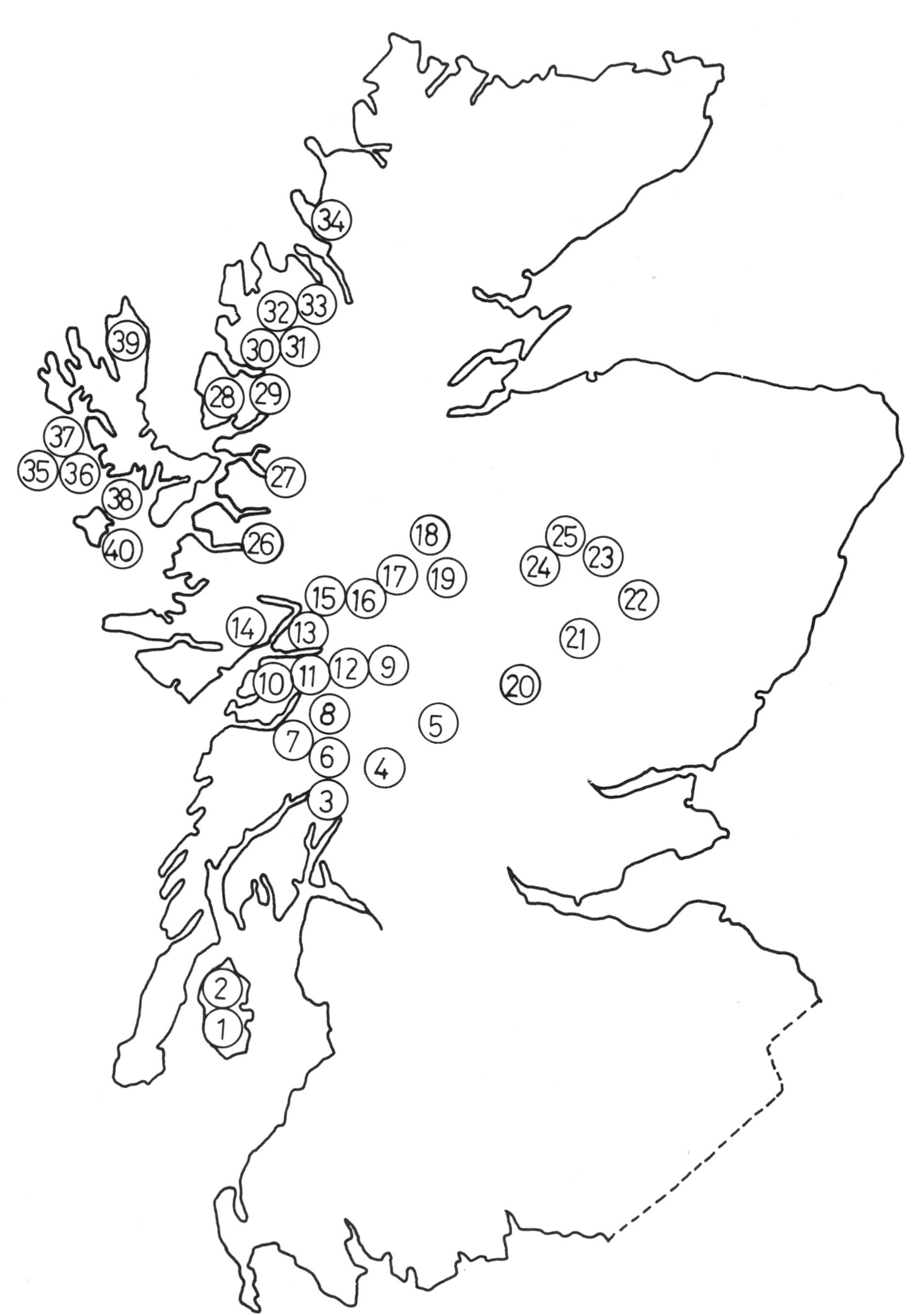
34
32
33
39
30
31
28
29
37
35
36
27
38
26
40
18
25
23
24
17
19
22
15
16
14
13
21
12
9
11
10
20
8
5
7
6
4
3
2
1

Scottish mountain climbs

Donald Bennet

B T Batsford Ltd · London

To Anne

who kept a light in the window
while we were on the hill

Frontispiece map *The numbers on the map refer to the relevant chapters*

First published 1979

ISBN 0 7134 1048 5

Filmset in 'Monophoto' Ehrhardt by
Servis Filmsetting Ltd, Manchester
Printed in Great Britain by
The Anchor Press Ltd, Tiptree, Essex
for the Publishers, B T Batsford Ltd
4 Fitzhardinge Street, London W1H 0AH

Contents

List of Maps

Acknowledgments

In mountaineering the companionship of one's fellow-climbers is as important as the climb itself, and I gratefully recognise the help given to me by many companions in gathering material for this book. In particular I am grateful to my wife, Anne and other members of the Bennet family, notably son John and cousin Arthur for their invaluable assistance.

Many fellow-members of the Scottish Mountaineering Club and the Scottish Ski Club have also contributed, sometimes unwittingly, and to them, particularly the ones who have balanced in precarious places while I fiddled with the camera, I send thanks. Some may recognise themselves in the pages of this book.

Finally, I acknowledge with thanks the assistance of Marion Simpson and Isabel Mungall with photographic work.

Introduction

One of the fascinating characteristics of Scottish mountaineering is the tremendous variety that there is in such a small country, only half of which is mountainous. There is variety in the mountains themselves, their shape and appearance, from the Cuillin of Skye with their jagged peaks and narrow ridges to the high arctic plateaux of the Cairngorms. There is variety too in the setting of the mountains, the backcloth against which they rise. In the west this backcloth is often the sea or the long and narrow sea-lochs which penetrate into the mountainous country; further east it may be vast and empty tracts of uninhabited moorland. Elsewhere the mountains rise among pleasant forested straths and glens with farms and woodland hugging their lower slopes.

Equally varied are the rocks from which the mountains have been carved by ice, rain and storm. Granite, gabbro, sandstone and schist; all have their own characteristics, their individual grain and texture which give shape and substance to ridges, buttresses, slabs and pinnacles. The rock-climber, like the geologist, acquires an intimate knowledge of these characteristics, but unlike the geologist, whose interest is scientific, the climber's interest in the roughness and toughness of rock is more personal, possibly a matter of life or death.

The mountains and rocks would, however, be stark and dull without the weather and seasons which invest them with light and colour, sunshine and shadow. Here too there is variety. We may not always speak kindly of our climate, but at least we should recognise that its many moods and vagaries clothe the mountains with an infinite variety of light and shade and subtle colours, and this is one respect in which the Scottish mountains are supreme. The seasons, too, bring their more dramatic changes of colour: the snows of winter, bright green of spring, the purple of high summer and the gold of autumn. To know the mountains in all these moods and colours we should walk and climb on them at all seasons.

The variety of the Scottish mountains is matched by the varied aspects of mountaineering that we can practise: hill-walking, rock-climbing, snow and ice climbing and ski-mountaineering. Each has its own enthusiasts, but just as no one can know the mountains completely in only one season of the year, so no one who confines himself to just one or two of these aspects can experience to the full all the adventure and beauty of mountaineering.

It is through hill-walking that most of us come first to the mountains, but the time when a couple of years hill-walking was regarded as an essential apprenticeship for all mountaineers is long past. Hill-walking in Scotland has a distinctive appeal for many thanks to the work of Sir Hugh T. Munro. His classification of the 3000 foot mountains and tops in his famous 'Munro's Tables' has put the sport of hill-walking on a formal basis, and for some has converted the very uncompetitive activity of hill-walking into a rather more serious business – Munro-bagging. The Munro-bagger, armed with a copy of the Tables, proceeds with unquenchable zeal and complete disregard for the weather from mountain to mountain and, if he is very keen, from top to top also, ticking off the summits as he passes them by. At one time the list of these who had 'done the Munros' was a select few, but now the number exceeds 150 and increases by a dozen or more each year. However, there can be no disputing the fact that those who qualify for the list have covered a lot of mountain country and gained a very great knowledge of the Scottish Highlands in the process.

Rock-climbing in Scotland has sometimes in the past appeared to be a sport polarised between east and west, a polarisation which reflected the character of the rock as well as the climber. In the north-east the Aberdonians have for years almost completely monopolised the granite of Lochnagar and the Cairngorms, and have acquired a reputation as tough as their native rock. Meanwhile the climbers of Edinburgh and Glasgow have co-existed uneasily in Glencoe and on Ben Nevis. Each group has for a few years dominated its own territory, the Etchachan Club in the north-east, the Creag Dhu and the Squirrels in the west, and each group has become particularly expert on its own crags. The Aberdeen climbers, for example, have acquired great proficiency in dealing with the vegetatious granite of their mountains, where every part of the anatomy – elbows, knees and eyebrows – may be needed to solve some tricky problem that might well confound a Glencoe climber accustomed to good clean rock. On the other hand, many an Aberdonian has been disconcerted at the tiny holds and steep walls on which a Glencoe climber would be quite at home, confident in the soundness of their tough volcanic rock.

It is in winter that the Scottish mountains really come into their own and assume their full stature, seemingly transformed by a covering of snow into giants twice their normal size. Climbs that in summer possess no great difficulty can in winter become serious undertakings of Alpine character, and difficult summer climbs may well become real test-pieces. In winter no route is ever exactly the same twice, for always there is something different in the snow and ice conditions that makes every winter climb to some extent a new route. In recent years the advances in Scottish ice-climbing have been spectacular. Modern equipment combined with confidence and skill on the part of the climber have produced routes of great difficulty carried out in remarkably short times, and Scottish ice-climbing now has a reputation far beyond this country.

Only in recent years has ski-mountaineering in Scotland developed from being the preserve of a dedicated few to become a respectable part of winter mountaineering. There are those, mostly young tigers, who say that ski-mountaineering is a sport for ageing climbers and skiers who have grown too old for the rigours of hard ice-climbing or downhill racing. Be that as it may, those who have left the crowded pistes and been converted to the langlauf way of life in middle age have renewed their youth in the glorious conjunction of skis, snow and mountains, and for them the joys of trudging around the hills in knee-deep snow have lost their attraction when compared with the exhilarating motion of the skier, particularly when he is speeding downhill.

Such then is the variety of mountains and mountaineering that Scotland has to offer. If this book has any purpose, it is to show this variety. The selection of mountains and climbs portrayed is certainly not intended to be any list of 'the fifty best climbs'. I would not presume to produce such a list. Rather, this is a personal selection of walks and climbs, scrambles and ski-runs which have never failed to give pleasure, and this is sufficient justification for their inclusion.

1 The Traverse of the Arran Peaks

The Island of Arran is set in the Firth of Clyde, and without doubt the beauty and character of the firth owe more to this grand island with its jagged mountain skyline than to any other feature. Even Alexander Nicolson, that ardent Skyeman and pioneer climber of the Cuillin, considered Arran to be the most delightful of the Scottish islands, though he did not go so far as to give the Arran mountains precedence over his beloved Cuillin.

The mountains of Arran are clustered together in the north-east corner of the island. There are twelve more-or-less distinct summits (if one excludes the far western hills which are lower and of less character), and two deep glens, Rosa and Sannox, penetrate into the heart of the mountains and separate Goat Fell and its neighbours (which rise steeply above the Firth of Clyde) from the other peaks (which lie over towards the west above Glen Iorsa).

There is a unique character about the Arran peaks which distinguishes them from all other Scottish mountains. The rock is granite which in many places has been weathered to form horizontal ledges and vertical cracks, giving the appearance of Cyclopean architecture. Where the granite is exposed on the mountainsides it forms huge areas of slabs, best seen on the face of Goat Fell above Glen Rosa. Along the ridges the granite has been weathered into rounded towers and narrow crests, and it is there that one sees the unique Arran mountain character at its best. The turf is short and springy, and narrow paths wind along the ridges, over and round the many towers, up and down little slabs and chimneys, full of variety and surprises. It is this delightfully varied character which makes the Arran peaks so fascinating for the ridge-walker. No one should let the reputation of the Witch's Step or the A'Chir Ridge with its 'bad step' deter him; these are the only difficulties that the walker will encounter on his way round the peaks, and there are ways to avoid them.

It is quite possible to traverse all the peaks in a single day, but this inevitably involves at least one long descent and reascent, and about 2500 metres of climbing. It is certainly easier to enjoy two shorter days, one on Goat Fell and its outliers, and the other on the long ridge west of Glen Rosa and Glen Sannox.

Starting the Goat Fell traverse at Sannox, one

1 *The A'Chir Ridge*

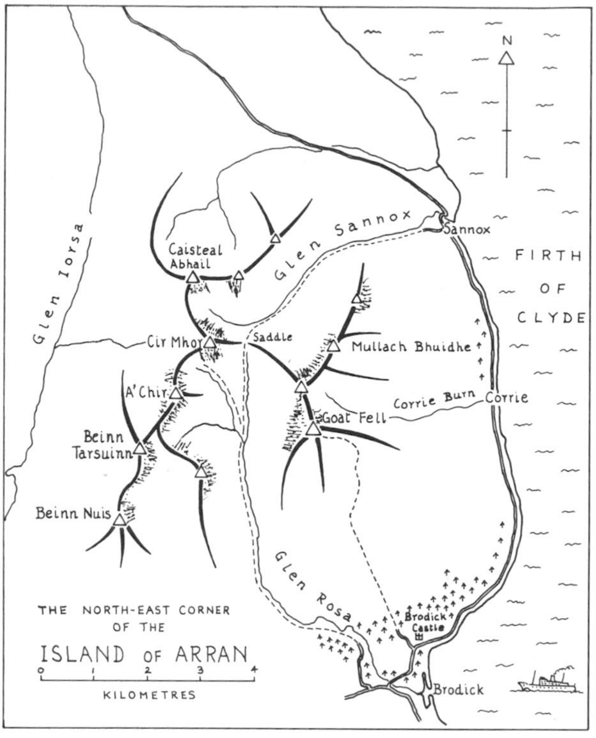

walks up the glen as far as the old mines before striking south-westwards across rising moorland towards Cioch na h-Oighe (661m). As the hill becomes steeper, so the path is more obvious, threading its way among the granite slabs and boulders on the north ridge. Higher up, this ridge becomes quite narrow, with an impressive drop into Coire na Ciche on its east side and long slopes falling steeply into Glen Sannox on the other side, and the path continues its airy way along the crest to the highest point. Proceeding southwards, the ridge becomes broad and grassy as it climbs towards Mullach Bhuidhe (819m), whose summit is the highest of several towers overlooking Glen Sannox. Beyond a wide grassy col one comes to North Goat Fell, and the final climb to Goat Fell (874m) goes along the castellated ridge called Stacach where there is plenty of scrambling if each little tower is climbed conscientiously, but there are also paths round the sides for those who prefer to walk.

Goat Fell, meaning the hill of the wind, is Arran's highest point, and on a clear day the view from the summit is one of extraordinary contrast. One can look east across the Firth of Clyde to the mainland coast where farmland and small townships are backed by low hills; then turning round one looks west to the wild ridges, peaks and corries beyond Glen Rosa. The descent by the well-worn path to Brodick provides yet more contrasts as one walks down through the tree-lined avenues of Brodick Castle.

The other half of the Arran peaks gives a longer and more interesting traverse, one of the best of its kind in Scotland. Again starting at Sannox, the first top – Suidhe Fheargha s (634m) – is soon climbed and the next peak is Ceum na Caillich, the notorious Witch's Step, a rocky pinnacle overlooking a narrow gap in the ridge. The steep descent to this gap involves some scrambling, first down a cleft in the summit rocks, then a little gully and finally a short smooth slab which is awkward to descend. The Witch's Step can be avoided by traversing round its north side, below the steep rocks of the pinnacle, to regain the ridge at the gap. From there the climb to Caisteal Abhail (859m) goes easily over and around a succession of little tors to the top of a large tor which is the summit of the peak.

Next on the ridge is Cir Mhor (798m), the finest of Arran's mountains, whose pointed summit seems to be the focal point where all ridges and glens converge. The north-east face drops precipitously into the head of Glen Sannox, but although this is the most impressive mountain wall in Arran, the combination of loose rock and heather detract from its climbing potential. Nearly all the climbing on Cir Mhor is on the Rosa Pinnacle, a superb buttress on the south face.

Continuing south-westwards from Cir Mhor, one soon reaches the start of the A'Chir Ridge, which everyone agrees is the finest part of the traverse. The ridge soon becomes narrow and exposed, and there is an awkward descent to a little col; on the south side of this col the crest rears up vertically and one has to traverse along a rising ledge on the east face until it is possible to climb directly up a short wall to reach the ridge again. A short distance further on, the crest becomes as narrow as a dyke, and one has to stride across a gap (the famous 'bad step') which appears sensational, but needs only a good head for heights. Finally, a succession of short chimneys and slabs brings one to the summit of A'Chir, which turns out to be a huge granite boulder, not entirely easy to climb without the aid of a shoulder. The descent along the southern half of the A'Chir Ridge is easier, but careful route-finding is needed if one is to avoid getting into difficulties on the slabby west face of the ridge. (The entire difficult section of the A'Chir Ridge can be avoided by following a path low down on the Glen Iorsa side.)

2 *Cir Mhor and Caisteal Abhail from North Goat Fell*

3 *Looking south-east from Caisteal Abhail towards Goat Fell*

The last part of the traverse takes one over Beinn Tarsuinn (825m) and Beinn Nuis (792m); the path meanders along the broad grassy ridge between the two peaks, but it is worth walking over to the edge of the ridge overlooking Coire a' Bhradain for there are impressive glimpses down the slabs of Beinn Tarsuinn, steeper and more intimidating than the Goat Fell slabs. Ben Nuis too has a steep eastern cliff just below its summit; it is the south-western outpost of the Arran mountains and the end of the ridge, but there are still many miles to go down Coire a' Bhradain and Glen Rosa to reach the civilised flesh-pots of Brodick at the end of the day.

4 *Scrambling on the Cyclopean granite of the A' Chir Ridge* (Photo: John Bennet)

5 *The Bad Step on the A' Chir Ridge*

2 The South Ridge of the Rosa Pinnacle

It was one of the interesting characteristics of the pioneer rock-climbers in Scotland (and no disrespect is meant, for they were mighty men) that they seem to have been attracted to some of the darkest, dampest and dirtiest gullies in our mountains. A case in point is the Ben Nuis Chimney in Arran; it was one of the earliest climbs done on the island, and was for many years the most notorious, not only for its difficulty but also for the loose rock and vegetation that lodged precariously in its dripping interior. In view of the reputation of the Ben Nuis Chimney it is a wonder that anyone went to Arran to climb.

In due course climbing fashions changed, and climbers turned their attention from dark gullies and chimneys to more open and exposed buttresses, ridges and slabs. Thus in Arran climbers began to look, as if for the first time, at the Rosa Pinnacle, a superb buttress of granite tapering to a slender spire for many years the most notorious, not only for its just below the summit of Cir Mhor. In 1933 J.A. Ramsay and his party made the original and very indirect route, and two years later they returned to climb the Layback Crack and thus complete the direct line on the upper half of the Pinnacle. In 1940

6 *The Rosa Pinnacle*

7 *The west face of the Rosa Pinnacle*

8 *The S-Crack*

9 *The Y-Crack*

Hamish Hamilton took up the challenge of finding a direct route on the lower half of the Pinnacle, but it took three visits with different companions – George Roger, David Paterson and lastly Bob Grieve – before he solved the remaining problems of the climb and established the South Ridge of the Rosa Pinnacle as one of the great Scottish rock-climbs.

As one walks up Glen Rosa and sees Cir Mhor for the first time, it is difficult, at a distance of five kilometres, to distinguish the Rosa Pinnacle from the slabby south face of the mountain. An hour's walk, however, brings one into the Fionn Choire and the Pinnacle is no longer hidden, but stands out boldly from the face of Cir Mhor, its features clearly seen – a broad base of easy-angled slabs, then a succession of steep walls girdling the front of the Pinnacle and finally its soaring, tapering spire; altogether 250m high. The key pitch of the climb is also obvious, the elongated S-shaped crack which is the only line of weakness in the lowest of the Pinnacle's encircling walls.

The climb starts without much difficulty up 60 metres of slabs with occasional steep little cracks and walls, aiming for the ledge below the S-Crack. Now the character of the climb suddenly becomes more serious, the wall above is smooth and vertical (or so it seems) and the appearance of the S-Crack is not reassuring; it looks like a pitch for a confident leader. It is indeed a great pitch which yields to determined climbing, feet jammed in the crack and hands pulling on its rounded edges. Excellent protection is possible with nuts placed in the crack, and a great moment comes near the top when the left hand stretches up to grasp a magnificent jughandle on which one can rest before the final pull onto the sloping ledge above.

There is no respite, for the next pitch, the Y-Crack, rises directly overhead, its last two metres overhanging slightly. Again determined climbing is called for until handholds on the slab above the overhang can be reached, but one must avoid jamming one's feet too securely into the crack just below the overhang. There are horrific stories of leaders who did just this and had to reverse the exposed crux to extricate their boots. (An escape from the hazards of the Y-Crack can be made by traversing right from the top of the S-Crack, round an awkward corner and along a broad ledge as far as the first groove on the east face. This groove leads back to the crest above the Y-Crack.)

The Rosa Pinnacle now relents slightly and one scrambles up slabs and boulders to the foot of the next encircling wall. The usual route is by the Layback Crack, which is gained by a rising traverse leftwards across easy slabs to a corner on the west side of the ridge. The long curving crack which springs from this corner is the Layback Crack, but the name is misleading for after two or three strong pulls a good resting place is reached, and from there (unless one chooses to continue up the crack) one can embark on a traverse rightwards. In contrast to the strenuous climbing below, this traverse calls for delicate balance as one edges across the slab on small footholds and no handholds, until the footholds disappear altogether and miraculously handholds appear higher up for the last part of the traverse.

The triple chimney above provides yet another contrasting pitch with more strenuous climbing, especially at the very top where one grasps the final chockstone and momentarily swings free over space before hauling up to safety.

Now the climbing becomes easier as one scrambles towards the topmost spire of the Rosa Pinnacle. It is possible to escape by continuing leftwards up a grassy terrace, but this would be an anti-climax. There is still some delightful climbing, first across slabs on the right where huge flake-holds make progress easy, then up a short chimney and right again across another slab to reach an airy stance on the crest of the Pinnacle. Finally an exposed traverse along a narrow ledge on the east face and a last pull-up bring one to the top.

Everyone who reaches the Rosa Pinnacle by the South Ridge knows well that he has had a unique experience; there is no other climb like it in Scotland. Nowhere else are there granite slabs and walls as clean and rough as those of the Rosa Pinnacle, nor pitches with the character of its three famous cracks; and for simple beauty that slender tapering spire has no equal.

10 *The Layback Crack*

3 The Traverse of The Cobbler

For most climbers the names Cobbler and Arrochar Alps are almost synonymous, for although The Cobbler (881m) is not the highest of this little group of mountains at the head of Loch Long, it is certainly the most distinctive. The strange outline of its three rocky peaks seen across Loch Long from Arrochar is one of the most dramatic mountain profiles on the Scottish mainland, and the great prow of the North Peak seems to overhang its base. The name Cobbler is rather fanciful as there is little resemblance in the shape of the mountain to a cobbler, but it seems to have originated over two hundred years ago when local folk, thinking that the appearance of the North Peak resembled a cobbler sitting at his last, called the hill 'an greasaiche crom', meaning the crooked shoemaker.

The traverse of the three peaks is a grand scramble, and there are many excellent short climbs on the North and South peaks. A classic traverse can be made by climbing the Recess Route on the North Peak, continuing to the South Peak and climbing it by the Direct Route. Both these Very Difficult climbs were pioneered by Jock Nimlin and his companions in the 1930s, a time of active exploration on The Cobbler when many young Clydeside climbers were seeking escape on the hills from the industrial depression of those days.

The traditional approach to The Cobbler takes the path (now rather overgrown) from Loch Long up the Allt a' Bhalachain (Buttermilk Burn), at first through birches and then recently planted spruce until the open hillside is reached and one comes to the Narnain Boulders. The first of these two boulders is the best known of the Cobbler howffs, and many climbers have spent cold, wet and draughty nights under its overhang. Nearby, the other boulder provides short practice climbs of all standards from quite easy to nearly impossible.

Beyond the boulders the path crosses the burn and climbs into the corrie under the three rocky

11 *Approach to The Cobbler by the Buttermilk Burn*

12 *Spectacular climbing on the North Peak*

peaks of The Cobbler. Eventually it goes close under the North Peak, and it is there, at the lowest rocks of the east face of the peak, that the Recess Route starts.

The Cobbler rock is Dalradian mica-schist of a contorted and folded structure and a silvery-grey appearance. It is this contorted structure that gives the striking outlines of the crags and peaks, and the folds provide plenty of little rounded holds.

Unfortunately the rock is extremely slippery when wet, and the climbs become considerably more difficult in these conditions.

The Recess Route starts up an easy-angled slab whose smoothly worn holds testify to the popularity of this climb. Above the slab the route assumes its true character, following a line of cracks, chimneys and caves in a series of excellent short pitches with

13 *A chimney on the Recess Route.*

14 *Exposure on Nimlin's Direct Route*

plenty of variety – some delicate climbing and some good old-fashioned thrutching. Half-way up a broad ledge is reached, and from its right end the crux pitch, the Fold, is climbed by small holds on its left wall until one can step rightwards to reach the top. There follow two short cave pitches and a scramble up to the foot of the steep wall just below the summit. The finish is up this wall, Ramshead Wall, by the line of least resistance to complete 100 metres of delightful climbing.

The outlook from the North Peak is spectacular as one is perched on the very edge of its great overhanging prow, but the traverse towards the Centre Peak is an easy walk. The summit of the Centre Peak, which is the highest of the three, is formed by a huge rock five metres high, and one must crawl through a window to reach a ledge on the south side of the rock and scramble up to the top. This is one of the most spectacular summits of any Scottish mountain, and one of the very few that can only be reached with a little rock-climbing.

The traverse continues down the narrow rocky ridge to the col below the steep face of the South Peak. To reach the foot of the Direct Route one must descend on the north side of the col until, about 30 metres lower, a quartz-studded ledge is reached which leads out across the steep face of the peak to the edge which forms its north ridge.

The Direct Route starts with a rising traverse along this ledge to the ridge, which is very steep and exposed at this point. A difficult pitch on the left side of the ridge leads to the easy middle section of the climb, where one scrambles up to the final upthrust of the ridge. The final pitch, delightfully steep and exposed, keeps close to the edge between the north-west and north-east faces, and ends right at the summit of the South Peak. This is an exhilarating climb whose exposure and airy situation are in marked contrast to the caves and chimneys of the Recess Route.

The South Peak is the least accessible of the three Cobbler peaks, with no easy routes to its top. The logical continuation of the traverse is down the south-east ridge, an easy-angled scramble of Moderate standard with a few short pitches leading to the foot of the peak and the end of the traverse.

15 *The summit of The Cobbler*

4 Stobinian and Ben More

Stobinian (1165m) and Ben More (1174m) are the most prominent mountains in the heart of the Southern Highlands, standing head and shoulders above their neighbouring peaks, and easily recognisable from many distant viewpoints. The only higher mountain in this part of Scotland is Ben Lawers, several kilometres distant to the north-east. The two mountains are like twins, not only nearly equal in height, but having the same conical appearance, particularly when seen from the north-west. Ben More appears to be the more massive mountain, an impression enhanced by the great sweep of its northern slopes over 1000 metres from Glen Dochart to the summit, and anyone climbing it from this side is bound to appreciate this character. Stobinian (or Stob Binnein to give its proper name) seems to be a more elegant peak, its ridges better defined and the tip of its cone cut off to leave a little plateau at the summit.

The two are very much hill-walkers' mountains, and the traverse from Loch Voil to Glen Dochart over their summits is one of the classic hill-walks of the Southern Highlands. It is not, however, one to be undertaken too casually in winter; the last part of Stobinian's south ridge is steep, and in hard conditions crampons or step-cutting may be needed. The descent north-westwards from Ben More is also steep, and there is a little hanging corrie just below the summit on this side of the mountain which should be carefully avoided if the snow is hard, or in a condition to avalanche. There have been some bad accidents at this point, at least one of them fatal, to remind one that even a relatively easy Scottish mountain must be treated with respect in winter.

Provided the conditions are right, Stobinian and Ben More are also grand skiers' mountains, and their ski-traverse is one of the best in Scotland. There may be some debate as to whether it is better to go from south to north, or the other way, but there is one very good reason for going from south to north – one skis off the summit of Stobinian down its north ridge, and this must be one of the finest ski-runs in Scotland. So let us take the traverse in this direction and hope for a clear day, for the pleasures of ski-mountaineering are largely lost, and the hazards greatly increased, if one is skiing unknown slopes in white-out or blizzard conditions.

16 *Ben More and Stobinian from Strath Fillan*

17 *Approaching Stobinian from the south*

Starting just beyond the head of Loch Doine, one climbs up Glen Carnaig on the west side of the burn, gaining height easily below the craggy side of Stob Invercarnaig until it is possible to turn westwards and reach the south ridge of Stob Coire an Lochain at a height of about 900m. This ridge is steep-sided, but the crest is wide enough and the angle of ascent easy enough for one to ski right up to Stob Coire an Lochain. Beyond this top the ridge becomes broad, though corniced on the east side, and one continues across a level col and up the steepening curve of Stobinian until a short distance below the summit skis come off and one may be glad of an ice axe for the last few steps to the cairn.

Now comes the highlight of the day – the ski-run northwards from Stobinian to the Bealach-eadar-dha Beinn, the pass between the mountains. One skis on the west side of the ridge, keeping well away from the cornice on the right and swooping to and fro down the open mountainside. Given good conditions (and this is always the big 'if' in Scottish ski-mountaineering) this is an exhilarating run, for the north-west face of Stobinian is steep and plunges

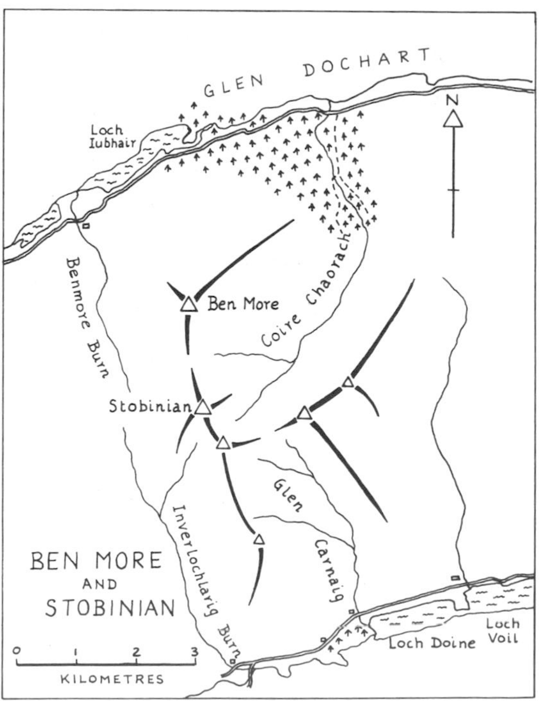

down over 600 metres to the Benmore Burn. All too soon, provided the temptation to keep on skiing downhill is resisted, the pass is reached and the uphill grind begins again. The climb to Ben More is probably steep enough for it to be easier to carry skis rather than try to zig-zag laboriously upwards on skins.

There is a certain challenge in standing on top of a hill and pointing one's skis down some untracked and possibly unknown ridge or corrie. On top of Ben More this challenge is obvious, for the mountain seems to drop on all sides in disappearing, ever-steepening slopes. There are, however, at least two possible routes. If one intends to return to the day's starting point at the foot of Glen Carnaig, the best plan is to ski back to the Bealach-eadar-dha Beinn, a more awkward and less pleasant run that the Stobinian descent. From the pass one can ski off eastwards into the level upper part of Coire Chaorach, contour round the foot of the east face of Stobinian and climb a short distance to the col at the head of Glen Carnaig. The long run down this glen

18 *Skiing down the north-west face of Stobinian*

makes a pleasant end to the day.

The traverse northwards from Ben More may be completed by skiing down the north-east ridge. This descent starts easily enough, but before long the ridge becomes narrow and rocky, and one has to make a cautious descending traverse below the crest on the north-west side; this is an exposed situation, for the slope below one's skis falls steeply for over 600 metres to Glen Dochart. Lower down, the ridge becomes broader and one can continue along the crest as far as the deer fence above the Ben More Forest. At this point it is probably best to ski eastwards into Coire Chaorach, keeping below the deer fence and looking out for a wide track which leads down through the forest on the west side of the corrie. This track gives an easy walk down to Glen Dochart, but woe betide anyone who fails to find it, for he may well become involved in an exhausting struggle bushwhacking through the densely planted trees of the Ben More Forest, and this would not be a good way to end the traverse!

19 *Looking back to Stobinian from the summit of Ben More*

5 The Ski Traverse of Ben Lawers

Ben Lawers has several claims to fame among the mountains of the Southern Highlands. For one thing, it is the highest, and taken with its six neighbouring hills it forms the biggest single group of mountains in the area. Although the name Ben Lawers applies correctly only to the highest peak, 1214m high, it is often used to include the whole range of seven distinct summits over 900 metres high. These summits are linked by a ridge 11 kilometres long which only once drops below 800 metres, and from them broad grassy ridges drop northwards to Glen Lyon and southwards to Loch Tay.

Ben Lawers can also be considered to be the birthplace of downhill skiing in Scotland, and at one time the quiet village of Killin could claim (with some justification) to be the leading Scottish ski resort. Long before the skiing boom which came in the 1950s, a fine winter weekend would see dozens, possibly even hundreds of skiers in Coire Odhar, and the Scottish Ski Club have had a hut in this corrie for many years. Since then, however, the downhill-only types have been lured away to the ski-lifts and bright lights of the newer centres, and nowadays relatively few skiers go to Ben Lawers, most of them being ski-mountaineers intent on reaching the high corries and summits rather than piste-bashing on the lower slopes.

In winter, when its smooth grassy slopes are well covered with snow, Ben Lawers is without doubt the ski-mountaineers' mountain *par excellence*. Among its many summits, ridges and corries there is a great variety of ski routes, from short and easy half-day tours to long and demanding traverses of the peaks. Typical of the shorter tours is the ascent of Beinn Ghlas from the car park at the foot of Coire Odhar. One can ski (or walk, depending on the snow line) easily up the west side of the Edramucky Burn to the Ski Club hut, and from there take an ascending line across the west flank of Beinn Ghlas to reach the little flat shoulder on its north-west ridge. The last

20 *Ben Lawers from Beinn Ghlas*

100 metres can either be climbed directly up this ridge, or by the slopes on its south side. In bad weather, when conditions make the summits impossible, a pleasant and very easy trip can be made by skiing from the car park to the Ski Club hut, and beyond it to the head of Coire Odhar and back.

The best ski tour on Ben Lawers is undoubtedly the traverse of the main ridge from Meall Corranaich to Meall Greigh, and this is one of the finest ski-mountaineering expeditions in Scotland. The skiing is always interesting, sometimes following the ridge and sometimes dropping down into the corries on one side or the other, and there is a constantly changing scene as one goes from peak to peak. This is, however, definitely a tour for fit and competent skiers, and more particularly for competent mountaineers, for it calls for good mountain sense and route-finding ability, especially in bad weather.

Starting at the north end of Lochan na Lairige, a short climb eastwards leads into the head of Gleann Da-Eig, and one skis easily up this open corrie heading south-east at first and gradually circling round north-eastwards to reach the first summit, Meall Corranaich. The easiest descent into Coire Odhar is down the south-west ridge for half a kilometre until the ridge becomes broad and level and one can turn off east and ski steeply down into the corrie. Continuing eastwards below the steep face of Meall Corranaich one comes to the foot of Beinn Ghlas and the route already described is followed to its summit.

In good conditions it is possible to ski down the crest of the north-east ridge of Beinn Ghlas directly to the Lawers-Ghlas col, and this is an exhilarating run. But beware, for the north-west side of the ridge is very steep, and at least one well-known Scottish skier has gone over the cornice in a white-out and finished up far below in a tangle of skis and poles, fortunately without serious results. In conditions such as those, or if there is not enough snow on the ridge, it is usually possible to ski down a broad shelf just below the ridge on its south-east side, but this takes one rather too low and it is necessary to climb back to the col. From there the ridge above is climbed to the summit of Lawers, on foot at first and then on skis higher up.

The second half of the traverse begins with a superb run from the summit, skiing northwards and keeping just on the west side of the main ridge to pass below the little rocky knoll called Creag an Fhithich and reach the Bealach Dubh at the foot of An Stuc. This fine peak is usually bypassed by skiers as its summit ridge is steep and narrow, and one can continue with a long descending traverse across its

21 *The ascent to Meall Corranaich from Lochan na Lairige*

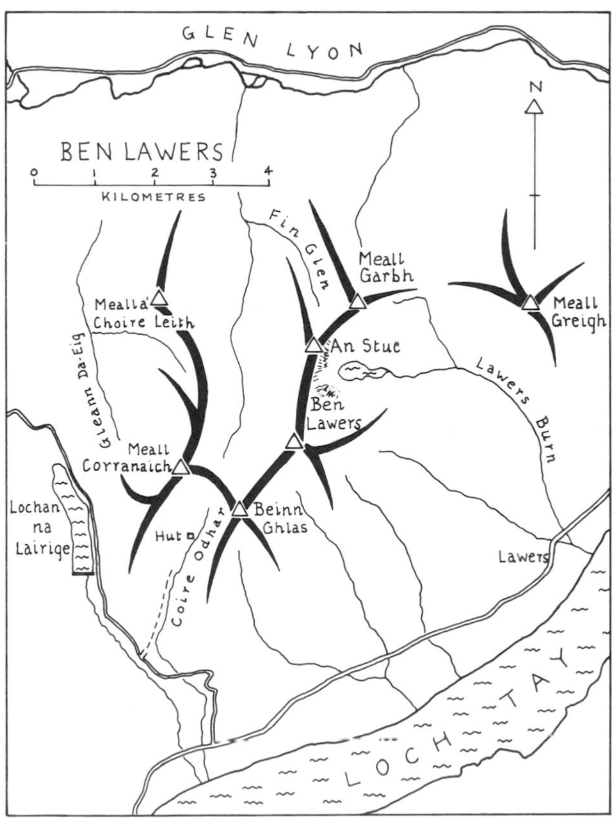

22 *Looking back to Meall Corranaich from Beinn Ghlas*

23 *Skiing off Beinn Ghlas towards Ben Lawers*

24 *Meall Garbh and An Stuc, and the northern corries of Lawers*

25 *Looking south-west from the summit of Ben Lawers towards distant Stobinian and Ben More*

west face, losing the minimum of height and arriving at the edge of the ridge overlooking the Fin Glen. There may be a cornice on the east side of this ridge which makes the first part of the descent exciting, but once below this obstacle there is an easy run down to the corrie where a huge boulder is a prominent landmark, and a good place to put on skins and draw breath before the 300 metres of climbing to Meall Garbh.

The best route is an ascending traverse north-eastwards to reach the north ridge of Meall Garbh, which is followed to the summit. The traverse continues along the north-east ridge for half a kilometre, and there is then another delightful ski-run eastwards to the col below Meall Greigh. This is the last summit of the traverse, and it is easily climbed by its broad west ridge.

The choice of route for the final descent will doubtless depend on snow conditions, one's aim being to ski as far as possible in the direction of Lawers village, looking for the lowest snow fields. The most direct choice is to point one's skis more or less due south towards Machuim Farm and take off. The first few hundred metres are steep, but lower down the slope becomes easier and the skiing more relaxed, provided of course that there is enough snow to cover the tufts of grass and heather. It would be a rare good fortune in the snowless winters of the 1970s to be able to ski right down to the road, but when it is possible it makes the perfect finish to a great day's ski-mountaineering.

6 The Centre Gully of Ben Lui

As one travels north-west from Crianlarich to Tyndrum on a fine day there comes a point just beyond the bridge over the River Fillan when suddenly a grand mountain bursts into view towards the west. The mountain is Ben Lui (1130m); it fills the head of the glen beyond Cononish and far overtops all its neighbouring hills. See it in winter or spring, when snow magnifies its size and the sun glancing across the mountainside gives shape to its ridges and corries, and then one may well think that Ben Lui, though not the highest, is in winter at least the grandest of the Southern Highland mountains.

The big corrie on the north-east side of Ben Lui is Coire Gaothaich, the corrie of winds, and snow lies in its high recesses until late in spring, long after it has disappeared from the surrounding hills. For the climber the most obvious challenge as he looks up at this face of the mountain is the direct ascent from the foot of the corrie up its headwall to the summit ridge; this is the line of the Centre Gully. First climbed in about 1891 at a time when Tyndrum was a rallying point for the early Scottish mountaineers, the Centre Gully has become the classic winter route in this part of the Highlands.

26 *Ben Lui from the north-east*

The best approach to Ben Lui is from Tyndrum or Dailrigh up the River Cononish and past Cononish farm. All the way up the glen one looks directly into Coire Gaothaich, and seen from this direction the Centre Gully appears remarkably steep, even vertical, like a curtain of snow hanging from the summit ridge of the mountain. However, appearances can be deceptive, and in reality the angle of the gully (except at the very top) is no more than 45 degrees. If the snow is soft the climb may be no more than a steep plod, but if conditions are hard or icy then the climb is an excellent one on which to learn the art of step-cutting or climbing on crampons. The last 50 metres are steeper, and there is often a big cornice which is quite an objective danger if a thaw is in progress. If freezing conditions prevail the leader may try tunnelling through the cornice, a strenuous and possibly suffocating operation that

27 *In the Centre Gully, looking towards Ben More and Stobinian*

will keep him warm for half an hour or so while the rest of his team shiver in their stances below. At the top of the Centre Gully, however, this tactic is seldom essential as the left hand side of the gully immediately below the summit is seldom corniced.

The climb ends within a few metres of Ben Lui's cairn, an excellent vantage point from which to survey the mountains of Argyll and Breadalbane. If the day is young the finest return to Dailrigh is over the summits of Ben Oss and Beinn Dubhchraig, and in the evening one can walk down through the pine wood at the foot of Coire Dubhchraig. This wood is one of the few remnants of the old Caledonian Forest in the Southern Highlands, and walking among these splendid old pines one can picture the Highland landscape as it once was before the forests were destroyed, and feel the timelessness which is symbolised by these ancient trees.

28 *At the top of the Centre Gully*

7 The Traverse of Ben Cruachan

Ben Cruachan (1126m), or more correctly Cruachan Beann, meaning the mountain of peaks, is well named for it is not just a single peak, but a long undulating ridge with short branches linking eight distinct tops over 900 metres. On its south side the mountain drops to the wooded shore of Loch Awe and its outflow through the narrow Pass of Brander. High up on this southern side of the mountain, in the corrie south-east of the highest top, is the upper reservoir of the Cruachan Pumped Storage Hydro-Electric Scheme, and in a huge underground cavern over 300 metres beneath the dam at the south end of this reservoir are the reversible turbine-generators of this remarkable power scheme.

The north side of Ben Cruachan overlooking Glen Noe is much wilder, and the narrow ridges which drop northwards from the three highest peaks enclose remote and seldom visited corries. In winter these ridges give good climbs, and there may still be scope for exploration among the crags and gullies of these corries where few routes have been recorded in the past.

The traverse of all the tops of Ben Cruachan is one of the classic hill-walks of Scotland. Nowhere is it

29 *On the Cruachan Ridge, looking towards the highest peak with Stob Dearg beyond*

difficult, but there are places, especially near the highest peak, where the ridge is narrow enough to give a feeling of exposure and exhilaration. Winter snow adds extra character to the ridge, which is often heavily corniced on its north side and in places has a positively Alpine appearance. A good starting point for the traverse is at the foot of the access road which goes from Lochawe up to the Cruachan Reservoir, and one can climb up the steep hillside northwards to the Monadh Driseig ridge and then turn west to reach Beinn a' Bhuiridh. Now comes the six kilometre ridge walk over a succession of tops – Stob Garbh, Stob Diamh, a short detour to Sron an Isean, Drochaid Glas, Ben Cruachan itself and finally Stob Dearg at the western end of the ridge.

As a viewpoint Stob Dearg is the best of the

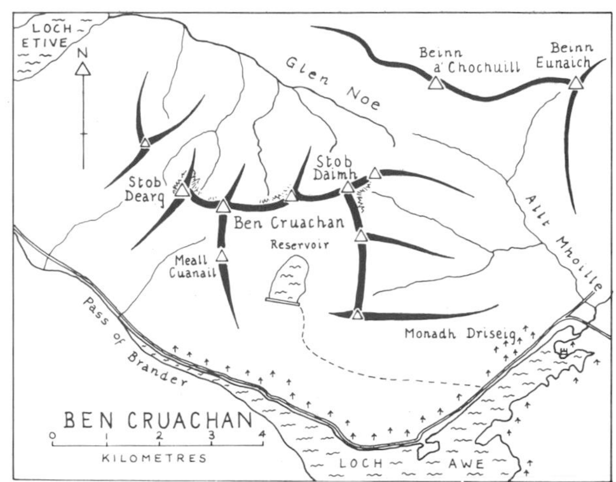

30 *Winter evening on Ben Cruachan; far below Loch Awe reflects the setting sun*

31 *On the Cruachan Ridge*

Cruachan peaks, for one is standing high above the narrow waters of Loch Etive, looking in one direction towards the distant head of the loch and the mountains of Glencoe and the Black Mount which surround it, and in the other direction towards the Firth of Lorn and the hills of Mull beyond. Mountains, loch and sea – these are the three essential elements which give West Highland landscape its special character, and from Stob Dearg one sees them in perfect setting.

The quickest descent is down the Allt Brander, but there is still Meall Cuanail to climb if one is to do all the tops. An easy descending traverse across the south-west side of Ben Cruachan leads to the col below Meall Cuanail; its ascent takes only a few minutes and one can continue in a south-easterly direction to the reservoir and on down the access road to the day's starting point at Lochawe.

Of several climbs which have been done in the northern and eastern corries of Ben Cruachan, one in particular has gained some reputation: the North Ridge of Stob Dearg. When this ridge was first climbed in 1892 the pioneers spent eight hours cutting steps up ice-covered granite slabs and boulders. The climb acquired an aura of difficulty at which modern climbers might scoff, forgetting that there is a world of difference between hob-nailed boots and crampons when it comes to climbing in hard winter conditions. Nonetheless, the North Ridge is a fine winter route, especially when (as on the first ascent) it is encrusted in ice.

An even better winter climb can be made on the steep north-east face of Stob Dearg. In summer the granite slabs appear too broken to be of interest, but in winter under a good plastering of snow and ice there are one or two good Grade III routes following the ledges and grooves which thread between the steeper sections of this face. To climb this face of Stob Dearg in winter is to experience the pleasure of exploratory climbing on a mountain wall that is steep enough to be challenging and has no well known trade route, so the climber must find his own way to the top. This is one of the great joys of winter mountaineering in Scotland.

32 *Looking towards the summit of Ben Cruachan from the west*

8 Climbs and Ski-Runs on the Black Mount

The Black Mount is the grand range of mountains which rises on the western edge of Rannoch Moor-mountains whose appearance must be familiar to all who travel the road north to Glencoe, for they dominate the western skyline all the way from Bridge of Orchy to Kingshouse Inn. Possibly the best impression of the range can be had from the road at the point where it crosses the River Ba; one looks westwards across the bare moor towards the lonely recesses of Coireach a' Ba and the long undulating crest of the Black Mount – Stob Ghabhar (1087m) on the left with its outlier Stob a' Choire Odhair standing in front, Clach Leathad (1098m) and Meall a' Bhuiridh (1108m) to the right.

There are other equally fine aspects of the Black Mount. The walk along the south-west shore of Loch Tulla through the pines of the Old Caledonian Forest is a beautiful approach to Stob Ghabhar, and from Kingshouse Inn the east face of Sron na Creise looks remarkably steep and forbidding.

The traverse of the Black Mount from Inveroran Inn near Loch Tulla to Kingshouse Inn has for years been one of the classic Scottish hill-walks. It could well be described as the best high level pub-to-pub

33 *The Black Mount*

traverse in the Highlands! In addition to the three main peaks of the Black Mount, several subsidiary tops can be included, and the crossing involves about 20 kilometres and over 1500 metres of climbing depending on how many peaks are included in the traverse.

High on the east face of Stob Ghabhar the rocky buttress just below the summit is split by a narrow gully – the Upper Couloir. When this gully was first climbed in 1897 by A.E. Maylard and his party, a landmark in Scottish winter climbing was reached, for the Upper Couloir and Gardyloo Gully on Ben Nevis (climbed in the same month) were the earliest recorded gullies in which the pioneers tackled steep ice pitches, earlier climbs having been entirely on snow.

For many years after its first ascent the Upper Couloir was regarded as a test-piece by aspiring Scottish climbers, marking the graduation from simple snow climbs to more difficult ice-climbing, where handholds as well as footholds had to be cut to maintain balance on the steep pitches. Now, however, the use of modern equipment such as front-point crampons and ice hammers has made step-cutting a declining art, and young climbers look for harder climbs to test their skills, but the Upper Couloir retains its reputation as a classic little winter route.

The climb is quite short; first, 50 metres of steepening snow as the gully narrows between its enclosing walls, then the famous ice pitch which varies in height between 10 and 15 metres according

34 *The east face of Stob Ghabhar*

35 *The ice-pitch in the Upper Couloir*

36 *At the start of the traverse, looking towards Stob Ghabhar from Meall a' Bhuiridh*

37 *At the end of the traverse, looking back from Stob Ghabhar to cloud-covered Clach Leathad*

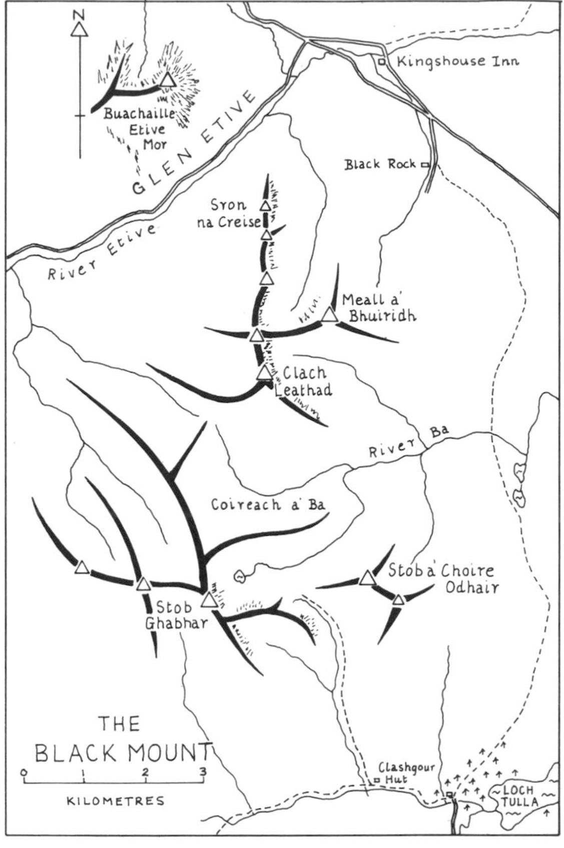

to the conditions and may be nearly vertical, and finally a steep snow slope leading to the ridge a few metres from the summit. It is not a difficult nor a particularly serious climb – about Grade II standard – but its remote position high on the steepest face of Stob Ghabhar gives it a fine character.

At the other end of the Black Mount, Meall a' Bhuiridh is one of Scotland's three main skiing centres, with a system of lifts and tows starting at the foot of the mountain and ending within a few metres of the summit. The north-east face of Meall a' Bhuiridh holds snow remarkably well and the runs, rejoicing in such names as Happy Valley, the Spring Run and the Flypaper, give some of the best downhill skiing in Scotland – the very best if one believes the local skiers.

The traverse of the Black Mount on ski from Meall a' Bhuiridh to Stob Ghabhar (or vice versa) is a very fine expedition, following the same route as the hill-walkers' classic traverse. The most popular direction is from north to south for the obvious reason that one can use the lift system on Meall a' Bhuiridh and reach its summit without any sweat. The descent to the col below Clach Leathad can be quite awkward, for the ridge is narrow and it drops steeply on both sides; there is little room for carefree skiing.

From the col a short steep climb on foot leads to the ridge at Mam Coire Easain a kilometre north of Clach Leathad, and one skis easily over this peak and a further kilometre along the ridge as it swings round towards the west. The southern side of this ridge is quite steep and rocky, and one must look for an open snow-filled gully which drops steeply for 200 metres towards the Bealach Fuar-chathaidh; in thick weather it may be a matter of luck to find the right place. The gully is very steep as ski-runs go, but in good conditions it can be skied; otherwise it may be more prudent to walk down the top half at least.

From the bealach there is a long and easy climb up the Aonach Mor ridge to Stob Ghabhar, three-kilometres distant. The final descent is down the south-east ridge; only the first part is at all hazardous, for one is skiing close to the cornice that overhangs the east face of Stob Ghabhar, and the consequences of a fall on this exposed part of the ridge are unpleasant to contemplate. Lower down the skiing becomes more relaxing, and provided there is enough snow a good run right down to the glen is possible.

The traverse in the reverse direction has some points in its favour. Once the long uphill grind from Loch Tulla to Stob Ghabhar is over, there is probably better downhill skiing when going in this direction; first the long run from the summit of Stob Ghabhar to the Bealach Fuar-chathaidh, and finally the descent from Meall a' Bhuiridh to the car park at the foot of the mountain. This descent is almost 800 metres, and if there is a complete snow cover it will probably live up to the claims made for it by the Glencoe faithful as being the finest ski-run in Scotland.

9 Summer and Winter on the Buachaille

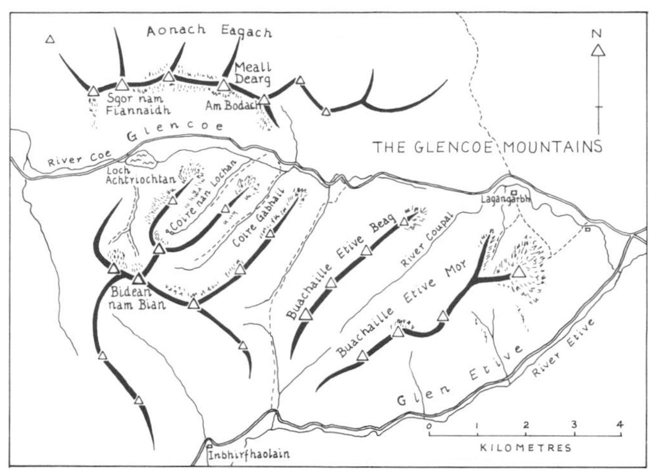

There can be few sights more familiar to Scottish climbers than the north-east face of Stob Dearg, the highest peak of the Buachaille Etive Mor (1022m), or just the Buachaille, to give the mountain its usual name. As one comes up the road from the south and tops the rise at the western edge of Rannoch Moor, so the mountain suddenly appears, its furrowed slopes rising beyond the furthest corner of the moor

38 *The Buachaille Etive Mor*

39 *On the North Face of Central Buttress, traversing right above Heather Ledge*

40 *Exposed climbing up the final pitch of North Face route*

41 *The first pitch of Agag's Groove. The climb continues up the very obvious groove*

in a pyramid of buttresses, ridges and gullies, all drawing the eye to the summit.

A few miles further west the road passes close below the peak of Stob Dearg, and on a clear day all its details are revealed. From the roadside one can see just about every chimney, groove, wall and slab of every route, with the possible exception of the dark caves of the Chasm and Raven's Gully. In winter one can look up into the recesses of Crowberry Gully and see if the pitches are banked up with snow or are showing dark ribbons of ice. The Buachaille hides nothing from its admirers below; it is a friendly, welcoming mountain, and few others inspire such feelings of affection. There must be many Scottish climbers who can look back at a hundred or more ascents of the mountain, in summer and winter, fair weather and foul. For them and many others a climb on the Buachaille is like a visit to an old friend.

The Buachaille is the supreme rock-climbers' peak. The rock is a rough and reliable porphyry, well provided with good little incut holds, particularly on its east facing cliffs of which Rannoch Wall – the east face of Crowberry Ridge – is the best known. It is on these steep walls, and in the cracks and grooves that are their lines of weakness, that one finds the most popular routes. Few of these routes exceed 120 metres, but it is possible to link them together to get more or less continuous climbs of 300 or 400 metres. One such combination of routes starts with Central Buttress, continues up Rannoch Wall and ends with the scramble up the top half of Crowberry Ridge to Crowberry Tower just below the summit of the mountain.

The early routes on Central Buttress belong to J.H.B. Bell; the North Face Route with A. Harrison in 1929, and the Direct Route and Central Chimney with C.M. Allan two years later; all Very Difficult. Despite many subsequent routes and variations, North Face Route has kept its reputation as a climb of great character and variety. In its lower section the route takes a course just right of the north-east corner of the buttress, but one must be careful. Go too far right and the climb deteriorates into a scramble; go too far left and the climbing becomes distinctly more difficult in the deceptively hard Kinloss Corner, whose well-scratched walls are evidence of many misguided climbers failing to get up and having to beat a retreat. The best part of the

42 *Typical Rannoch Wall climbing, steep and exposed, on January Jigsaw* (Photo: John Bennet)

43 *Crowberry Tower, where many routes on the Buachaille converge just below the summit*

44 *The Buachaille in winter*

45 *Crowberry Gully in winter. The Thincrack Chimney completely choked with ice* (Photo: K. Crocket)

climb comes above the Heather Ledge where one traverses right onto the north face. There follow in quick succession a short vertical wall, a steep chimney and (if Douglas Scott's excellent variation is taken) a traverse left to the edge of the buttress and a final pitch of superb rough slabs direct to the top.

Rannoch Wall is the epitome of Buachaille climbing: steep and exposed, yet well supplied with good holds which enable routes to be made in the most unlikely looking places. Certainly there are some very hard routes, but there are also easier ones; the ambience of the wall is sunny and the climbing not too serious. Curved Ridge provides a gallery from which spectators can encourage performers on the wall while eating their sandwiches and waiting their turn to climb.

This was the scene one sunny day in August 1936 when Hamish Hamilton and his companions, Alex Anderson and Alex Small, made the first ascent of Agag's Groove, having beaten Bill Mackenzie's rival party by a few minutes in the race to the foot of the climb. Agag's is the obvious line of weakness on Rannoch Wall, a long groove starting at the lowest point and curving across the wall to end below the vertical upper rocks. It was a bold lead, for there was a fair amount of loose rock which inspired the name of the route (Agag was the biblical character who trod delicately), and above the groove the upper part of the wall is very exposed. Hamilton dealt with these problems in typically ebullient fashion, throwing down loose rocks to the alarm of his companions and the spectators below. Nowadays Agag's Groove is the trade route on Rannoch Wall, and has even been described by one guidebook writer as the most useful route of descent on the wall, but neither of these descriptions can detract from its character.

There are other routes more typical of the steepness and exposure of Rannoch Wall. January Jigsaw, Satan's Slit and Red Slab were all products in 1939 and 1940 of the short climbing carrer of H.I. Ogilvy, a career which ended tragically a year or two later in a fall on Sgoran Dubh. His Rannoch Wall climbs were a significant step forward, however, for they follow very tenuous lines of weakness and are continuously steep and exposed. At the stance which January Jigsaw and Satan's Slit share below their final pitches one is perched on the edge of a void, and grateful for the steel spike which has served as a belay for over 30 years, a tribute to Clydebank steelwork.

In winter the focus of climbing on the Buachaille shifts to the other side of Crowberry Ridge. By common consent the best winter route on the mountain is Crowberry Gully, not on account of any great difficulty (although it may be Grade IV), but rather for its beauty and character, its impressive situation enclosed between the walls of Crowberry Ridge and North Buttress, and not least because in snowless winters it may be one of the few routes on the mountain in condition. The first ascent of Crowberry Gully was made by Harold Raeburn and E.W. Green in April 1898, but despite the season it was not a true winter ascent, and the first winter ascent seems to have been that of Bill Mackenzie and Hamish Hamilton (partners now, not rivals) with Kenneth Dunn and J.B. Russell in February 1936.

In winters of heavy snowfall the first three or four pitches may well be obliterated, as they were on the occasion of the 1936 ascent, and then a steep corridor of snow leads up into the heart of the gully. In these conditions the first pitch of any consequence comes at mid-height, and it is usually climbed by an icy groove on the right wall followed by a traverse back into the bed of the gully. An ever-steepening ribbon of snow leads to the next pitch, the notorious Thincrack Chimney, but in winter there is no possibility of climbing inside the chimney – which is invariably choked with ice – and one has to make do on the slabby right wall.

Immediately above, Crowberry Gully forks and the crucial part of the climb is at hand. The situation at this point is impressive, for the gully is deeply enclosed between steep walls and it is obvious that there are only two ways to go – up or down. Escape is impossible. The normal route goes up the right fork, but the problem may well be how to get into it, for there is a slabby barrier to be passed. If the slabs are well plastered with ice the route goes that way, starting at the foot of the left fork and traversing rightwards and upwards to reach easier ground. If there is inadequate ice on the slabs it may be necessary to resort to a more devious route, climbing the left fork for a few metres, traversing rightwards over a little spur and dropping down into the right fork above the slabs.

Once in the right fork the last pitch is not far away, a 15 metre cave whose right wall is often a frozen cascade of ice. Technically it is the hardest thing in the gully, and to cut steps up the ice-wall may be very time-consuming, although one has the comforting knowledge that once up there are no more difficulties. Another comforting thought may be that there is a possible escape route just below the cave, a traverse rightwards onto North Buttress, but no one would ever admit to its existence. However, there have doubtless been parties, weary after hours of climbing and facing the possibility of a night out, who have been glad to use it. On the other hand, there are some climbers who consider that no Scottish winter route is complete without a torch-lit epic on the last pitch and a descent in darkness. For them Crowberry Gully is the climb *par excellence*.

10 The Etive Slabs

Glen Etive is one of the most delightful of Scottish glens. As one passes Kingshouse Inn there is the impression of this glen disappearing south-westwards among the mountains; its road leads nowhere, so most tourists press on northwards. Yet as soon as one turns off the main road and passes Coupal Bridge the character of the glen is felt; on both sides the mountains rise abruptly, the Buachaille on one side and the Black Mount on the other, and between them the river plunges on its course to Loch Etive through narrow gorges and foaming cascades. All along the river there are grassy campsites and bathing pools among the rocks.

From the head of Loch Etive one looks up at the side of Beinn Trilleachan where there is a vast expanse of pale slabs; these are the Etive Slabs. Many years ago there must have been a huge landslip which carried the whole hillside – heather, trees and boulders – down to the edge of Loch Etive, leaving exposed the bare granite of the mountain – a few acres of smooth slabs at an angle of about 45 degrees.

Dozens of climbers must have been in Glen Etive without realising the potential of the Slabs. From the head of the loch distance and foreshortening tend to diminish their scale and steepness. Only in 1954 did Eric Langmuir and Mike O'Hara make the first routes – Sickle and Spartan Slab. When others heard, a rush followed, and between 1957 and 1960 ten more routes were added, all Very Severe and most of them the work of Mick Noon with John Cunningham and other Creag Dhu climbers.

Since then the popularity of the Slabs has rivalled, and possibly even exceeded that of the long established Glencoe crags. There are good reasons for this, the most obvious being that the climbing is superb, if you like slab climbing. The approach walk from the pier at Loch Etive is only twenty minutes, and being at low level and facing south-east the Slabs get plenty of warmth and sunshine, certainly more than the Glencoe crags. Long before the high mountains are snow-free in spring, and long after the rock-climbing season is traditionally thought to be over,

46 *Glen Etive. Looking from the Slabs towards the mountains round the head of the glen*

47 *Climbers on the Slabs dwarfed by the scale of their surroundings*

48 *The view from Spartan Slab towards Ben Cruachan*

the Slabs may be warm and dry. This long climbing season is disturbed in August by the ferocious activities of the midges, which on the windless and humid days that seem to characterise that month are out in force and can repel climbers as effectively as the rain.

The Slabs are deceptive. One might think, taking a foreshortened view from below, that friction alone would be enough to get one up; but this is very far from the case, for the granite is smooth and quite literally holdless for much of its expanse, so that a great deal of faith and determination are also needed. Even the obvious corners which might be expected to give lines of weakness often turn out to be no easier than the slabs. As a result most routes on the Slabs are serious propositions, long and sustained, and calling for confidence, commitment and two very different styles of climbing: delicate movement on the tiny wrinkles of the slabs and strenuous pull-ups and honest thrutching to surmount the overlaps and steep walls which surmount them.

Spartan Slab might be considered the *voie normale* of the Etive Slabs, a mixture of slabs, cracks and grooves, and a good introduction to harder things. Although graded Very Severe, it is low in this class and liable to be demoted to Severe in the next edition of the guidebook. One might say of it, as the Creag Dhu used to say disparagingly of any new route by a rival party: 'Aye, maybe it's V.S., but it's no fierce.' There is a big coffin-shaped boulder at the foot of the rocks where all climbers foregather to eat lunch and change their boots; it is the social centre of the Slabs. Spartan Slab starts close by and trends away to the right, avoiding the smooth central sweep of slabs and breaking through the first overlap near its right end, where a huge chunk of granite has detached itself and slipped downwards half a metre to leave a slit up which one thrutches.

Higher up a hand-traverse leads rightwards to the edge of the slabs and the only way is up by steep cracks, over a bulge and on to easier ground. The last pitch, a groove which looks straightforward from below, turns out to be more awkward than it seems and so the interest is maintained right to the end, where the climb finishes among little trees and a series of short vertical walls. Then it is back to the coffin stone to sort out gear, have lunch and consider the possibility of another climb or just a swim in Loch Etive.

49 *The crux pitch of Spartan Slab*

11 Summer and Winter on Bidean nam Bian

The south side of Glencoe is filled by the peaks, ridges and corries of a single great mountain, Bidean nam Bian (1141m). The most familiar appearance of Bidean is that of its three projecting ridges – the Three Sisters – which tower above Glencoe, and from the depths of the glen it is these three peaks which fill the view. The higher summits seem remote and withdrawn, standing above the innermost recesses of their corries, far behind the outlying peaks.

Bidean is one of the most fascinating mountains in Scotland, truly a mountaineer's mountain, and there is a great variety of walking and climbing among its many peaks and ridges, cliffs and corries, both in summer and winter. It is a mountain which cannot be 'done' in a day or two; rather it takes many visits and many days of exploration before one can claim to know it completely: summer days climbing on the steep walls of Aonach Dubh and Gearr Aonach, winter days on the buttresses and gullies of Stob Coire nan Lochan and Stob Coire nam Beith, and days of wandering in the corries and along the ridges.

The topography of Bidean encourages the climber who enjoys an upward progression of rock-climbs, interspersed with walking, which lead eventually to one of the summits. For example, one could start by walking up into Coire Gabhail, better known as the Lost Valley, and spending an hour or so exploring the caves and scrambling on the boulders which have been left by a huge rockfall from the side of Gearr Aonach. Then an ascending traverse up grassy rakes on the north-west side of the corrie brings one to the foot of a very steep face 100 metres high, where there are delightful routes of Very Difficult standard: Mome Rath Route and The Wabe. These climbs have never gained great popularity, and they still share the tranquility and silence of the Lost Valley. They end on the level grassy ridge of Gearr Aonach close to the upper part of Coire nan Lochan.

50 *In Glencoe, looking up towards Gearr Aonach and Aonach Dubh*

51 *On the East Face of Aonach Dubh*

52 *At the head of Coire nan Lochan, below Stob Coire nan Lochan* (left) *and the South and Centre buttresses* (right)

53 *Front-pointing on the first pitch of S.C.Gully* (photo: K. Crocket)

The walk up the lower part of Coire nan Lochan takes one below the East Face of Aonach Dubh, one of the pleasantest crags in Glencoe; superb rock and plenty of sunshine on a good summer day. When Bill Murray made the first routes on the East Face in 1947 he said of them: 'On the East Face all men may climb.' His remark is as true today as it was then, for although many new routes have been added in the last 30 years (some of extreme difficulty) there is still a complete spectrum of routes and something for everyone to climb.

The lower half of the cliff is, at its highest part, a rather featureless convex wall which is very steep at its foot and not over generously provided with holds where they are most needed, so that the principal routes – Weeping Wall, Long Crack and Curving Crack – are all Severe. There are, however, easier lines further left. The upper half of the East Face has a fine central wall bounded on its left by a dark curving chimney. On this wall there are three excellent routes: Quiver Rib, Arrow Wall and Archer Ridge. No one could possibly complain about the lack of holds on these routes, and although they are short (no more than 80 metres) they give superbly steep and exposed climbs of Difficult to Mild Severe standard.

An uphill walk across the side of Aonach Dubh brings one to the heart of Coire nan Lochan where three buttresses soar high above the tiny lochans. The rock architecture in this high corrie is quite different from the lower cliffs; the rock is andesite with a distinctive columnar structure, forming slender pillars and narrow grooves, and giving the buttresses a cathedral-like appearance.

For many years these buttresses were neglected in summer, most climbers probably thinking that there was not enough good rock to repay the long walk up to the corrie. It was only in 1961 that their true potential was realised when Ken Bryan and Roger Robb climbed Central Buttress by a Very Severe direct route of 150 metres, starting at the toe of the buttress and following a series of grooves to the top. More recent routes on South Buttress are of extreme difficulty, and the reputation of the corrie for summer rock-climbing is now established.

On the other hand, the reputation of Coire nan Lochan for winter climbing has long been established, and it is one place where good climbing conditions can normally be expected, even in fairly mild winters which leave other parts of Glencoe damp and snowless. Like the East Face in summer, Coire nan Lochan in winter gives climbs of all standards. At the easy end of the scale there are Broad Gully (more popular as a descent route), N.C. Gully and the narrow ridge of Dorsal Arête. Higher up the scale there are three Grade III routes that are Glencoe winter classics: S.C. Gully, Twisting Gully and Central Buttress.

At one time S.C. Gully had a considerable reputation for difficulty, and was the test piece in Coire nan Lochan. Now this reputation has rather diminished as harder climbs have appeared, but still S.C. is a worthy route; short, but very steep and impressive, for the gully is a deep slit between its bounding walls. There are usually two ice pitches, a short steep one at the foot of the gully and a longer one at mid-height, where the route is up a raised shelf on the right side of the gully. Conditions, however, can be very variable; in the great winter and spring of 1947 Bill Murray found the lower half of the gully to be an almost continuous 70 metre ice pitch, but that was exceptional and it seems more usual in recent mild winters to find a lack of ice rather than a surfeit. Despite this, S.C. Gully is probably the most popular winter route in the corrie, and a very early start is needed on a good winter day if one is to avoid being second or third party up the gully, and at the receiving end of a hail of snow and ice chips.

On the other side of the South Buttress, Twisting Gully is a very different type of climb. The difficulties are not steep ice (unless a direct ascent by the right fork is taken), but short and awkward pitches on snowbound rock, particularly low down in the gully where one traverses left along an obvious ledge before climbing directly up. Good hard snow can simplify these pitches, whereas in soft snow they may be quite unpleasant.

54 *Looking east from Bidean towards the Buachailles*

The third of the Coire nan Lochan winter classics is Central Buttress, by Raeburn's ordinary route and not Bryan's direct route. At its foot there is a big corner between the face of the buttress and a projecting spur. The corner is climbed to the crest close to a small pinnacle, at which point one discovers that a much easier way lies up the N.C. Gully side. Thereafter one continues directly up the crest on mixed snow and rock, making short right traverses where direct progress is impossible. It is a pleasant climb, but not too serious, for escape is possible into N.C. Gully.

All these climbs end on the north ridge of Stob Coire nan Lochan, and on a fine day it is a great moment as one cuts through the cornice at the top of a sunless gully and steps into the brilliance and light of a winter afternoon. On such a day one is reluctant to leave the heights, and there is an urge to stay up on the mountain for as long as possible. The ridge-walk over Stob Coire nan Lochan to Bidean, the highest peak of Argyll, is a good postscript to any climb, and one may be rewarded by one of the great views of Scotland. To the north Ben Nevis stands high above his neighbours and eastwards are the many tops of Buachaille, but it is to the south that the eye is drawn, towards the shimmering waters of Loch Etive and the distant peaks of Starav and Cruachan.

On the top of Bidean there is all the feeling of being on a high mountain, remote and withdrawn, surrounded by lesser peaks and far above the valleys. It is a place to linger until chill winds and approaching night drive one down towards Coire nam Beith or the Lost Valley, down to the shadowy depths of Glencoe.

55 *The summit of Bidean nam Bian*

12 The Traverse of the Aonach Eagach

There is a marked contrast between the mountains on the opposite sides of Glencoe. Whereas Bidean nam Bian on the south side is a mountain of many peaks, ridges and corries, the Aonach Eagach is a single narrow ridge enclosing the north side of the glen like a high wall. The name, meaning the notched ridge, is appropriate as the ridge has many ups and downs over little peaks and pinnacles, with narrow gaps between them. The three kilometre ridge between Sgor nam Fiannaidh (967m) and Am Bodach (940m) is in places as narrow as any of the mainland ridges.

In summer the traverse of the Aonach Eagach is a good scramble, but it poses few difficulties and anyone with modest rock-climbing ability and a good head for heights will romp along with no bother at all. In winter, however, the traverse is a more serious undertaking altogether, with snow and ice providing a variety of problems and the additional factor of short hours of daylight to take into account.

It makes little difference whether one goes from east to west or the other way, but the east-west traverse has the slight advantage that the climb to Am Bodach from the Glencoe road near the Meeting of the Three Waters is short and easy compared with

56 *Am Bodach at the eastern end of the ridge*

the long slog up Sgor nam Fiannaidh from the foot of the glen. From Am Bodach the traverse starts with a short and steep descent which is often awkward in winter, but then the ridge continues easily to Meall Dearg (951m).

The section west of Meall Dearg is the best part of the ridge; it is narrow and exposed and swings up and down with occasional short pitches. The highlight is the airy traverse over two little pinnacles at the narrowest part of the ridge where an impressive drop on the north side makes the difficulty more apparent than real, but it is a place where many climbers are glad of a rope. There are a few more steep pitches as the ridge drops towards the col, but there all difficulties end. Finally an easy climb to Stob Coire Leith (939m) and a walk along the ridge, now broad and level, brings one to Sgor nam Fiannaidh, the westernmost and highest peak.

Although the Aonach Eagach, even in winter, can hardly be described as a difficult climb, it has a reputation for benightments. Many parties have found

57 *The middle part of the Aonach Eagach where the ridge is narrowest*

the mid-winter days too short, or their own pace too slow, to complete the ridge in daylight, and at nightfall watchers in the glen below can see the torch-lights flashing high up on the ridge. In such circumstances there is a strong temptation for climbers on the ridge, facing the possibility of a cold night out, to attempt to descend to Glencoe by one of the many steep gullies on the south side of the Aonach Eagach. This is a temptation to be resisted, for most of these gullies have steep pitches, unseen from above, and it is more prudent to continue to one end of the ridge or the other where descent routes are easier.

There are, however, climbers who would delight in the prospect of a night on the Aonach Eagach, and the winter traverse by moonlight is a unique experience in Scottish mountaineering; it is also a very rare experience, when one considers the probability of good snow conditions, good weather and a full moon combining to make it possible.

58 *Looking west from Stob Coire Leith towards Sgor nam Fiannaidh*

13 The Mamores Traverse

Between Loch Leven and Glen Nevis there stretches a long mountain chain, the Mamores, whose ten separate peaks are linked by a switchback ridge, itself about 16 kilometres long. The Mamores are definitely hill-walkers' mountains, for once on top one can walk for miles from peak to peak; the traverse of them all is the best day's ridge-walking in the Central Highlands, a glorious succession of summits with intervening ridges linking them in a series of sweeping curves. On all sides the mountain flanks are scalloped into innumerable corries, large and small, and in many of these corries old stalkers' paths (few of them still used for their original purpose) give easy access to the ridge.

Spring is the best season for the Mamores traverse, for then the days are long enough for many miles of ridge-walking, and with luck there will be snow on the peaks to enhance their graceful contours. Indeed, a fine spring day in the Mamores, with blue skies and sparkling snow, is the nearest thing there is to perfection in Scottish hill-walking, and such a day more than makes amends for the many others betweentimes when we are beset by rain, wind and cloud. Although many have done the

59 *The eastern end of the Mamore ridge, dominated by Binnein Mor*

60 *On the south ridge of Sgurr a' Mhaim*

traverse, few if any have repeated the marathon hill-walk of Philip Tranter who in 1964 traversed the Mamores eastwards from Polldubh, descended to the watershed at the head of Glen Nevis and returned westwards to his starting point along the crest of the Grey Corries, the Aonachs and Ben Nevis, all within twenty-four hours.

Mullach nan Coirean (939m), at the western end of the Mamores, is flat-topped and probably the least interesting of the peaks. Going eastwards, Stob Ban (999m) is very different; its pointed summit, precipitous north-east face and the white quartzite screes which give the peak its name make this one the most distinctive of the Mamores. There is some

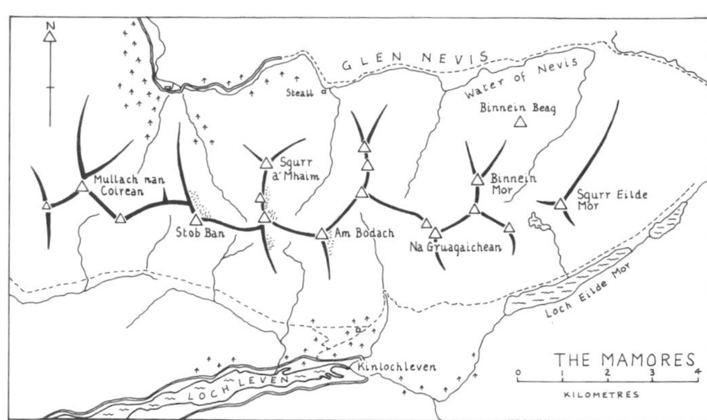

61 *The Devil's Ridge*

62 *The summit of Binnein Mor*

63 *Descending from Binnein Mor towards Na Gruagaichean. In the distance the Glencoe mountains are deep in shadow*

good winter climbing on the buttresses and gullies of the north-east face.

Continuing eastwards, the next top is the flat summit of Sgor an Iubhair (1001m), but this is just the junction of the fine ridge which runs northwards for a kilometre to Sgurr a' Mhaim (1098m). This ridge should not be missed, for it is one of the best bits of the Mamores: halfway along it becomes very narrow and exposed, and this part is called the Devil's Ridge. Though not difficult in summer, in winter the ridge may be more formidable if it is corniced and icy, and in these conditions it has a very Alpine appearance.

From Sgor an Iubhair the main ridge curves gracefully onwards to Am Bodach (1043m) and Stob Coire a' Chairn (983m), where another northward spur leads to the twin summits of An Gearanach and An Garbhanach. Then there is a low col and about 300 metres of climbing to the two tops of Na Gruagaichean (1055m). As one approaches the eastern end of the Mamore ridge, so the grand peak of Binnein Mor (1128m) appears more and more to be the outstanding mountain of the whole group. It is like a great wedge; from the west the summit seems to be a short level ridge, but as one comes over the south top, so Binnein Mor becomes a sharp-pointed peak, its south ridge forming the narrow edge between steep sides. Little wonder that it is considered to be the finest of the Mamores.

There remain two peaks beyond Binnein Mor and separated from it by low cols; they are Sgurr Eilde Mor (1008m) and the little cone of Binnein Beag (940m). They stand on opposite sides of the deep Coire a' Bhinnean in which rise the headwaters of the River Nevis, and the hill-walker who has to climb them both to complete the traverse will have to consider carefully which one to do first; the decision will no doubt depend upon whether he intends returning to Glen Nevis or Kinlochleven. Either way, there are still 600 metres of climbing and some rough country to cross before one of the paths leading down to the valley is reached.

14 Two Climbs on Garbh Bheinn

There is a special feeling about crossing Loch Linnhe at Corran Ferry and setting foot in Ardgour; it is the feeling of crossing the sea to reach the true western part of Scotland, a region more akin to the islands than the rest of the mainland. Indeed, Ardgour, with its neighbouring districts of Morvern, Sunart and Ardnamurchan, is almost cut off from the mainland by those long narrow lochs – Linnhe, Shiel and Eil.

On a clear day at Corran Ferry one's eye is drawn westward beyond the intervening ridges to the tip of a splendid looking mountain, Garbh Bheinn (885m). Though not the highest peak of Ardgour, it is the finest, and its bold outline gives some hint of the grand ridges and buttresses which rise above Coire an Iubhair on the east side of the mountain.

On the approach up this corrie Garbh Bheinn is at first hidden, and one has to walk some distance before the east face of the mountain begins to reveal itself – first the slabby north and north-east buttresses at the head of the glen, then the blunt towers of the Pinnacle Ridge and finally the Great Ridge, a superb pillar of rock directly below the summit. These are the most striking features of the mountain,

64 *Garbh Bheinn*

but elsewhere in the corrie there are slabs and crags in profusion, the rock is a coarse grey crystalline gneiss, and Garbh Bheinn certainly lives up to its name – the rough mountain.

The Great Ridge is the most obvious route for the rock-climber – a narrow tapering ridge whose base is encircled by steep slabs and whose crest soars up to the summit of the mountain. The first ascent was made by J.H. Bell and W. Brown in 1897, but their route avoided the lowest part of the ridge by a rising traverse from the south-east up a shallow gully and across steep grass. In 1952 Dan Stewart and Donald Mill discovered the Direct Start to the ridge which, linking up with the original route, gives a superb 300 metre route of Difficult standard with one Very Difficult pitch, the first.

This first pitch of the Direct Start is an obvious line of weakness in the lowest wall of the ridge, a steep crack between dark overhanging rocks on the left and paler slabs on the right. For twenty metres the crack is steep and the climbing sustained; then the angle eases and one scrambles up to a grass ledge. Now the route continues more easily by steep walls, but so plentiful are the holds and so rough the rock

65 *Superb scrambling on the Great Ridge*

66 *The North-East Buttress of Garbh Bheinn*

67 *On Route Two; high above is the smooth expanse of Leac Mhor and above it the overhanging face of the Turret*

that one can choose one's own line up to the broad grass ledge below the ridge proper.

At its start the ridge is very narrow, a mere knife-edge, and there is the sensation of tight-rope walking as one tip-toes up the airy crest. On the second pitch a short steep chimney gives more strenuous climbing. Now the ridge steepens and although there is a tendency to traverse onto the left flank where the rock is easier, the best climbing for the next 50 metres is right on the crest where there are some good moves and that feeling of exposure which all good ridge climbs have. Gradually the rocks become easier and one scrambles upwards, until suddenly the summit cairn is reached and there is nothing more to climb.

The North-East Buttress is quite different in character from the Great Ridge; it is a broad buttress of slabby rock, 400 metres high, overhanging in places and crossed by grass ledges so that there seem to be four tiers. An obvious feature is the huge smooth slab which forms the third tier; named Leac Mhor (the great slab), it is the heart of the buttress and its intimidating appearance is accentuated by the overhanging rocks of the Turret which surmount it. Such is the character of the North-East Buttress that early climbers sought the lines of least resistance, true mountaineering routes. This was certainly the case for the first two climbs done, unimaginatively named Route One and Route Two.

Both climbs start at the foot of the easy-angled grey slabs which form the lowest tier, and there are two pleasant pitches followed by scrambling to reach the first grass ledge. On the second tier Route Two is near the left side of the buttress. One climbs to a ledge below a prominent overhang and then traverses rightwards, until a steep climb directly upwards leads to the second ledge.

The great slab Leac Mhor is now directly overhead, guarded along its base by an overhanging wall. Only at one point is this overhang pierced, at an open corner, and by it one can reach the lower edge of the slab at the foot of a long shallow chimney. This is the only line of weakness, for on both sides the slab seems smooth and unclimbable, and it is in fact the key to Leac Mhor. Fifty metres up, the chimney widens and a huge chockstone is jammed in it; at this point alternative routes diverge.

The original route, climbed by B.K. Barber and J. Lomas in 1939, leaves the chimney and embarks on a long upward traverse to the right across Leac Mhor. Although not difficult, there is a lack of protection and a feeling of isolation and exposure about this pitch, and by the time he has climbed to the full

extent of his rope the leader will be glad to find a belay. At the end of the traverse a short steep wall is climbed and the original route continues rightwards, circumventing the overhanging side of the Turret by easier slabs. Dan Stewart made a fine variation in 1952 by leaving the original route just above the steep wall, traversing left onto the front of the Turret and climbing directly upwards.

Two years later a slightly more direct route was made by Len Lovat. Continuing up the chimney beyond the chockstone, an overhung recess is reached where the second man can belay in a superb eyrie at the top of Leac Mhor, with overhanging rocks above and smooth slabs plunging below. The leader moves up leftwards across a grey slab sparsely supplied with holds, traverses delicately round its edge and disappears up a steep groove. This is the crux, for the next pitch, a steep and narrow groove on the left side of the Turret, turns out to be easier than it looks and beyond it the route degenerates into a scramble up the roof of the Turret. The Direct Finish, with its one Severe pitch, is certainly harder than the original route and the Turret Variation, both of which are Very Difficult, but its difficulties are concentrated into a single pitch and there is more good climbing on the Turret Variation.

Above the Turret all routes merge, taking a direct line up the front of the tower which forms the final tier. There are no difficulties to compare with the lower pitches, but the climbing is a steep and satisfying finish to a grand route which has taken one to the heart of the North-East Buttress to discover the secrets of the Leac Mhor.

68 *Out of the shadow into the sunshine; a traverse on Route Two*

15 Ben Nevis, the Supreme Mountain

Ben Nevis is the one Scottish mountain which merits more superlatives than any other: it is the highest, its rainfall is also reputedly the highest and its weather the worst; however, to compensate for these climatic disadvantages, it has the biggest cliffs with the longest routes, and in winter the climbing is the nearest thing we have to Alpine mountaineering.

The walker on the 'Tourist Path' from Glen Nevis to the summit will appreciate the first, and possibly the second and third of these characteristics, but he is unlikely to appreciate the grandeur of the cliffs of the north face unless he looks over the edge of the plateau, which may be extremely hazardous if the cornices are melting in spring and early summer. Anyone wanting to see the north side of the mountain should, on a fine day, walk round to the glen of the Allt a' Mhuillin and climb Carn Mor Dearg. From the summit of this peak one has a magnificent view of the whole north face of Ben Nevis and its great cirque of ridges, buttresses and gullies. The day should be completed by continuing along the Carn Mor Dearg Arête (photo 69), the narrow yet perfectly easy ridge which curves round to Nevis (photo 70) and gives the hill-walker his finest approach to the mountain.

The salient features of the north face are Tower Ridge and the North-East Buttress, two splendid ridges 600 metres high which rise from the Allt a' Mhuillin to the summit plateau. Both were climbed by the Hopkinson brothers in September 1892, and were the first climbs done on the Ben, although 50 years previously local peasants climbed up to the little snow-fields which lingered throughout summer in the gullies to collect blocks of ice for fish-curers in the valley. The opening of the West Highland Railway in 1894 brought more climbers, members of the Scottish Mountaineering Club for their Easter Meets in 1895 and 1896, and a steady procession of climbers ever since. Some more than others have left their mark: Harold Raeburn with his many climbs, including solo ascents of Observatory Ridge and Buttress; Graham Macphee, the dedicated guidebook writer who drove up from Liverpool at weekends to climb on the Ben; Brian

69 *The Carn Mor Dearg Arête*

Kellett, the solitary climber who made a remarkable series of hard solo routes in the 1940s; Jimmy Marshall, who has done more on the mountain than any other climber and whose one week campaign with Robin Smith in February 1960 raised Ben Nevis winter climbing to its present level.

In summer the rock-climbing possibilities of Ben Nevis are strangely neglected, and the corrie (normally alive in winter with aspiring ice-men) is often empty and silent. There are reasons for this neglect, for Nevis weather is notoriously bad and the rock becomes very slippery when wet, so anyone going there in summer is taking a chance, but if he is lucky with the weather his reward will be great. There is a tremendous pleasure and satisfaction about climbing warm dry Nevis rock on routes of great length and character; often the only other climbers in the corrie are one's own companions, and on a long midsummer day it is possible to do 1000 metres of climbing before the sun leaves the mountain.

The two best rock-climbing cliffs on Ben Nevis are the north-west face of North-East Buttress, the Orion Face, and Carn Dearg Buttress which overlooks the C.I.C. Hut at the lower end of the corrie. The former is the huge slabby wall rising 400 metres above the foot of Zero Gully, and its history is linked with one man in particular – J.H.B. Bell. It was he who with various companions in the early 1940s achieved the constellation of climbs that inspired the name Orion Face. The trade route (if such a cliff can be thought to have a trade route) is the Long Climb, and its character typifies the face: long pitches on sound yet slabby rock, a feeling of serious mountaineering and the need for route-finding skill, and above all the awe-inspiring ambience of this steep and sunless mountain wall.

Carn Dearg Buttress has a very different character. Its front, 250 metres high, is a great expanse of steep overlapping slabs; the rock seems rougher and the holds less rounded than elsewhere on the Ben, and on a fine morning it is flooded with sunshine. The fact that there are no climbs on the buttress less than Severe is no disadvantage but rather an added attraction as far as modern rock-climbers are concerned, most of whom go for the big direct lines such as Bullroar, Centurion and Sassenach. Lesser mortals need not be deterred from Carn Dearg Buttress, for there is in Route Two (one of Kellett's climbs) a fine route which seeks the line of least resistance diagonally across the buttress.

Starting at the bottom left hand corner, two long pitches on superb rough slabs followed by a dark

71 *Clouds drift across the north face of Ben Nevis, throwing into relief the North-East Buttress and Tower Ridge*

72 *The C.I.C. Hut and Carn Dearg Buttress*

vertical chimney lead up the left side of the buttress. Then a long exposed traverse rightwards takes one into the centre of the cliff to the grassy recess under the upper overhangs. Continuing the traverse under the overhang, one reaches the outer edge of the buttress and two more pitches, exposed but not unduly difficult, lead to the top. Route Two is a superb climb; technically Very Difficult, its Severe grading is probably justified by its length, exposure and serious character, for it would be very difficult to retreat from high up in the event of a rain storm.

It is in winter, however, that Ben Nevis reveals its true character as the supreme Scottish mountain. Under a plastering of snow and ice the three great ridges, Tower Ridge, Observatory Ridge and North-East Buttress, become climbs of truly Alpine character, and the steep gullies such as Zero and Point Five are the yardsticks by which young ice climbers measure their skill and stamina. (Ian Nicholson has done them both before lunch, but that is exceptional.)

73 *On the first pitch of Route Two on Carn Dearg Buttress*

74 *An exposed traverse on Route Two*

75 *The Great Tower*

76 *The Eastern Traverse*

Although many climbs tend over the years to lose their reputations, there are others that keep theirs. The great Nevis ridges are examples of climbs which have never been down-graded in climbers' eyes, and one can be assured of a good struggle on them any winter. Of the three it is Tower Ridge that seems to have the greatest fame, not because it is the most difficult, but rather for the quality of its difficulties which come as a climax to the route, near its end. Many parties have climbed to within 100 metres of the top only to suffer defeat or benightment, and Bill Murray has vividly described the hazards of the last part of the ridge late on a December afternoon with darkness falling and the wind rising.

Tower Ridge starts easily enough with an ascent of one of the gullies leading to the Douglas Boulder Gap, but the short chimney leading from the Gap onto the ridge is often awkward. The ridge continues narrow and level for some distance, and the next rise is usually best tackled by a traverse rightwards along a steeply banked snow ledge until the snow-covered rocks above can be climbed. The next difficulty is the Little Tower where a couple of pitches of steep snow-covered rock have to be climbed, and the leader must be particularly careful, as a fall at this point could leave him dangling in space over the edge of the ridge. Another easy section with one surprisingly awkward step leads to the foot of the Great Tower and the start of the real difficulties.

The usual route round the Great Tower is the Eastern Traverse. In summer this is a comfortable ledge two feet wide along which one walks without concern. In winter deeply-banked snow may obliterate the ledge altogether so that the leader is faced with a long traverse across an extremely steep and exposed wall, hopefully plastered with hard snow, for soft snow on the traverse would be very nerve-racking if not downright dangerous. Beyond the traverse the route continues up a little groove (where the tunnel of the summer route is blocked with snow), and onwards by a rising traverse to regain the crest of the ridge just beyond the summit of the Great Tower.

The summit plateau now seems close at hand, but there is still one obstacle to cross – the Tower Gap. It is at this point, where the ridge is a mere knife-edge of wind-blown snow, that a storm can make life very difficult, for one is completely exposed to the elements and has the very strong impression that a sudden gust of wind could easily hurl the whole

77 *The last pitch; reaching the summit of Ben Nevis at the top of Observatory Ridge*

78 *The summit cliffs of Ben Nevis. Two climbers about to cross the Tower Gap*

party into the depths of Tower Gully. The crossing of the gap is greatly simplified if (following the example of Bill Murray) one can cast the rope across and lasso a spike of rock on the far side, but usually snow hides the spike and more conventional tactics are needed. The leader must drop down into the gap and climb out the other side, possibly by a little groove on the left side of the ridge.

Once the leader is established on the crest above the gap the party can relax, for except in very unusual circumstances there are no more problems. The last part of the ridge is straightforward, but as one wearily cuts the last few steps and hauls oneself over the little cornice onto the summit plateau there is the sure feeling of having just done a great climb. Depending on the conditions one may be tempted to describe it as the hardest, the most beautiful or simply the most enjoyable of one's Scottish experience.

16 The North-East Ridge of Aonach Beag

Aonach Beag (1236m) is the second highest mountain in the western half of the Highlands, yet it is relatively unknown and seldom climbed. No doubt its higher neighbour, Ben Nevis, attracts most of the attention of climbers in Lochaber, and other mountains are neglected by comparison. There is also the fact that Aonach Beag is quite remote, and is hidden from most viewpoints to the north and west by Ben Nevis and the nearby high peaks of Carn Mor Dearg and Aonach Mor; only from the south and east can one appreciate its great bulk rising above Glen Nevis.

In its features Aonach Beag resembles Ben Nevis on a slightly smaller scale. Both mountains have the same flat summits and precipitous north-east faces. The finest feature of Aonach Beag is its North-East Ridge which rises 500 metres from the headwaters of the Allt a' Chul Choire to the summit plateau. In its middle part the ridge is steep and rocky, broken into little pinnacles and as narrow as a knife-edge.

The earliest recorded ascent of the North-East Ridge was made by J. Maclay, W.W. Naismith and G. Thomson in April 1895, but for the next 50 years the climb remained almost totally neglected, with

79 *The east face of Aonach Beag, with the North-East Ridge directly above the skier*

80 *Below the first pinnacle on the North-East Ridge*

only a handful of ascents. Even today the remoteness of the North-East Ridge seems to have preserved it from popularity; yet it is just this quality that is the great fascination of the ridge, and the climber setting out for it does so in a spirit of exploration, knowing that somewhere on the distant side of the mountain, in its remotest corrie, there is this unknown route calling him. Truly it is a climb for those seeking mountain solitude, one which is best done in spring when there is enough snow on the ridge to give it an Alpine ambience, and transform its upper part into a succession of snowy crests.

Any approach to the north-east side of Aonach Beag is long, and the best one is probably that which starts at the road-end in Glen Nevis. At first one

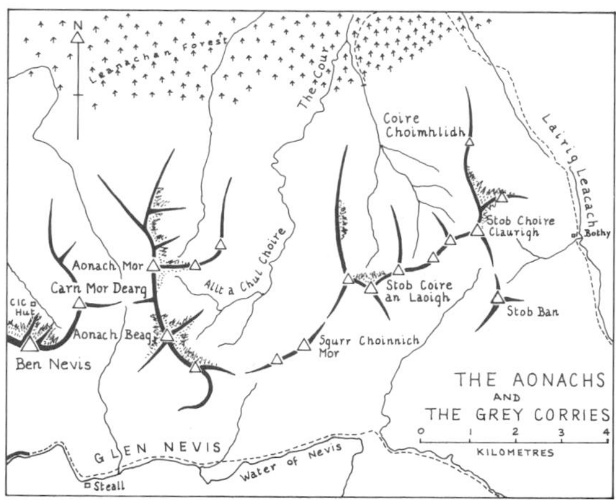

81 *The upper part of the North-East Ridge*

82 *The summit of Aonach Beag. The last part of the North-East Ridge forms the left hand skyline*

climbs through the beautiful Nevis gorge, where the path clings to the steep wooded hillside and the River Nevis plunges through the boulder-strewn ravine below. Then suddenly one emerges from this narrow pass into the more open space of the upper glen, where the river flows less turbulently and the path leads eastwards towards the distant watershed. Two kilometres beyond the ruined cottage at Upper Steall an easy climb northwards leads to the col between Sgurr a' Bhuic and Sgurr Choinnich Beag, and from there one can see at last the day's objective – the North-East Ridge. It soars from the depths of the corrie to the summit plateau, and an almost level traverse below the face of Aonach Beag leads to its foot.

The lowest part of the ridge is broad and much broken up, so that one can climb easily for a hundred metres or so. Then the crest becomes steeper and narrower, and is barred by two little pinnacles; the climbing begins to look more serious, especially if conditions are icy. Traversing round the north side of the pinnacles, the ridge is regained below a short overhanging nose, and again (unless a direct attack up this overhang is contemplated) a traverse, this time on the south side, is made for a short distance until the ridge can be regained above the nose. Now the crest is a true knife-edge, spectacular if snow covered and giving a wonderfully exposed scramble until it becomes broader again, and one can climb easily up the last 100 metres to the cornice which guards the summit of Aonach Beag.

By comparison with the great ridges and buttresses of Ben Nevis, which on a clear day dominates the view westwards, the North-East Ridge is altogether an easier and less serious route; however, the pleasure of climbing it comes not so much from the technical difficulty of the climb as from the feeling of isolation and exploration, of having penetrated to the remotest corner of the Lochaber mountains to discover Aonach Beag.

17 The Ski Traverse of the Grey Corries

The range of mountains which extends eastwards from the Aonachs towards Loch Treig is known to the Gaelic-speaking folk in Glen Spean as Na Coireachan Liath – the Grey Corries. This is an apt description of these peaks in summer at least, for at that season their appearance is characterised by the pale grey quartzite screes of their ridges and corries.

At the western end of the range Sgurr Choinnich Mor is a beautiful pointed peak, comparable to Binnein Mor on the opposite side of Glen Nevis. The central section of the Grey Corries is the three kilometre ridge from Stob Coire Easain to Stob Choire Claurigh, and further east, beyond the Larig Leacach, are the twin peaks of Stob a' Choire Mheadhoin and the other Stob Coire Easain.

In summer these mountains give pleasant but unexciting hill-walking. In winter they are transformed by snow, which enhances the sweeping lines of ridge and peak and the rounded hollows of their corries. Then the Grey Corries become hill-walkers' country *par excellence*, with the lonely bothy in the Larig Leacach giving primitive shelter in the heart of the mountains.

Although the Grey Corries are not generally

83 *Skiing off Stob Coire Easain towards Sgurr Choinnich Mor*

84 *On the ridge of Beinn na Socaich*

85 *Superb ski-touring conditions on the Grey Corries*

86 *On the main ridge of the Grey Corries near Stob Coire an Laoigh*

known as skiers' mountains, there is some excellent ski-touring on them, particularly in the central section. The ridge from Stob Coire Easain (1080m) to Stob Choire Claurigh (1177m) is ideal for a ski-traverse provided there is a good snow cover; it is narrow enough to be interesting without being unduly difficult. On the north side of the ridge the wide expanse of Coire Choimhlidh gives superb downhill skiing when it is packed with snow.

Possibly the best starting and finishing point for the traverse is at the foot of Coire Choimhlidh, where a private road ends near a little dam on the Allt Choimhlidh. From there one can make either a clockwise or an anti-clockwise circuit of the peaks; the standard of the skiing is the same in both directions.

Going anti-clockwise, one climbs easily towards the north end of the ridge called Beinn na Socaich. Although the Ordnance Survey map shows this ridge as having a narrow crest, it is in fact quite broad, and one can ski easily right to the summit of Stob Coire Easain. On a clear day there are magnificent views westwards towards the Aonachs, with Ben Nevis appearing above the col between them.

The crest from Stob Coire Easain to Stob Choire Claurigh continues up and down over four intervening peaks, including Stob Coire an Laoigh (1115m), the second highest point on the ridge. At one or two places it is possible to ski northwards off the ridge into Coire Choimhlidh, but this should only be attempted with caution. From Stob Choire Claurigh the first few hundred metres of the north ridge are narrow, and are best negotiated by a careful descending traverse on the west side just below the crest. Then the ridge becomes broad and one can continue easily northwards towards Beinn Bhan.

There may, however, be better skiing if (after the narrow section of the ridge) one makes a descending traverse south-westwards into the head of Coire Choimhlidh. Now the full length of the corrie lies below, and after the cautious skiing up on the ridge there is an exhilarating freedom in this vast white arena, choosing one's own route down shallow gullies and schussing across virgin snowfields. It is this discovery of new and untracked runs that is one of the great pleasures of ski-mountaineering.

18 Winter Climbs on Creag Meaghaidh

The highest peak on the north side of Glen Spean is Creag Meaghaidh (1130m), a large and complex mountain from whose summit plateau several ridges drop towards Loch Laggan and its westward extension, Loch Moy. The easiest ascent is on this side, possibly up the ridge on the west side of the Moy Burn, but anyone going to the summit and returning by this route will miss the best part of Creag Meaghaidh. The grandest feature of the mountain is Coire Ardair where, one and a half kilometres east of the summit, the plateau ends abruptly and huge precipices drop to the lochan lying in the depths of the corrie below.

Coire Ardair is the mountain's chief attraction from the climbers' point of view, and the usual approach is from Aberarder farm, following the path along the north side of the Allt Coire Ardair. At first this path leads upwards through scattered stunted birches until, rounding the corner of the glen, one sees the corrie three kilometres ahead. The main features of Coire Ardair are the Pinnacle Buttress on the south side, and on its right, seemingly forming the headwall of the corrie, the great Post Face, so named after the three posts or gullies which are its

87 *The Coire Ardair face of Creag Meaghaidh*

obvious features. To the north of the Post Face the cliff curves round westwards to form an inner corrie leading towards the prominent col, the Window, on the north side of Creag Meaghaidh.

As so often in the early days of Scottish climbing, Harold Raeburn was the first to explore the climbing possibilities of Coire Ardair, but on an April day in 1896 he and his companions were chased from the foot of the Centre Post by avalanches. This is a reception which the corrie seems to reserve for many of its visitors, particularly in spring, and over the years the Posts have gained something of a reputation for their avalanches. On this occasion Raeburn and his companions climbed the easy gully on the left of the Post Face and reached the Pinnacle from the west. In 1903 a second attempt to climb the Centre Post by Raeburn, this time in summer conditions, was foiled when he reached a huge pot in the upper part of the gully which was running with water and filled with spray; obviously it was not a summer climb.

Many years passed before serious attempts to

88 *The snow-bound cliffs of Coire Ardair*

89 *The edge of the Creag Meaghaidh above Coire Ardair*

90 *Near the top of the North Pipe, Staghorn Gully*

climb the Posts were renewed, and this time J.H.B. Bell was the driving force. In 1934 he and his party climbed the long slanting gully to the right of the Posts (named Staghorn Gully many years later), and in March 1937 with C.M. Allan he climbed the Centre Post. It was a *tour de force* even though the huge pot, transformed in winter into a vertical 60 metre ice pitch, was avoided by an excursion to the right of the gully.

Twenty years later the South Post was climbed by Malcolm Slesser and Norman Tennent, the North Post fell soon after to Tom Patey and his party, and so by 1960 Coire Ardair became established as second only to Ben Nevis in the Central Highlands as a winter climbing centre. Being high, remote from the mild winds of the Atlantic and facing north-east, the corrie can usually be relied on to give good winter climbing, but the avalanche hazard should not be ignored if snow conditions are soft or a thaw prevails.

Possibly it was the increasing popularity of Coire Ardair that inspired one group of Glasgow climbers to build their own hut in the corrie. On the first attempt a small portable cabin was carried up to the lochan, but it lasted only a short time before the winds removed it. The second attempt, a tiny stone hut built behind a huge boulder under Pinnacle Buttress, has proved to be more enduring, but so inconspicuous is this hut that to find it on a dark winter night is problematical.

Centre Post is the winter trade-route in Coire Ardair. It is a climb on a grand scale, 400 metres high and having all the ambience of a great route taking, as it does, a direct line up the middle of the Post Face. In a winter of heavy snowfall the lower half of the gully is more in the nature of a steep snowfield, and several short ice pitches (which are evident in snowless winters) are obliterated. Then the gully narrows and is barred by the huge 60 metre ice pitch. The usual route, following Bell and Allan's original line, escapes rightwards from the gully by a shorter ice pitch and a long rising traverse, until a return leftwards along an exposed snow gallery leads back into the gully above the great pitch. This pitch was led by Brian Robertson in 1964, but it is considerably harder than anything else on the climb, Grade V as compared with Grade III. At its top Centre Post debouches into a wide snow basin below the cornice, and it is easy to imagine how powder snow, driven across the plateau by a west wind, can accumulate in this basin and occasionally crash down the whole length of the gully.

Staghorn Gully has the advantage of being a safer

91 *Skiing westwards from Creag Meaghaidh towards the head of Glen Roy*

climb when conditions are uncertain. There is no difficulty in following one of the two parallel snow ramps which end high up on the north-east corner of the cliff. Immediately above is the South Pipe, an ice-filled chimney which is the hard way to finish the climb. The easier and more popular finish is the North Pipe, a narrow gully reached by traversing further right for about 30 metres; it is about 100 metres high, and has at least one, more usually two, short ice pitches before it emerges onto the snowfield below the cornice.

Centre Post and Staghorn Gully are typical of the middle standard (Grade III) routes in Coire Ardair. There is a wealth of other winter climbs, almost all of the gully variety, hard and easy, to keep the climber busy for many winters. Finally, anyone tiring of gully climbs can try part or all of Tom Patey's Girdle Traverse, a remarkable route over two and a half kilometres long following ledges, sometimes broad and sometimes narrow to the point of nothingness round the entire cliff-face of Coire Ardair. It is unique among winter climbs in Scotland.

19 Ardverikie Wall

Binnein Shuas is a modest hill on the south side of Loch Laggan, which, with its twin neighbour Binnein Shios, hides the remote strath in which lie the Lochan na h-Earba. This is one of the quiet and beautiful corners of the hills between Lochaber and Badenoch, frequented more by fishermen than climbers.

Not until 1964, so it seems, did climbers discover the big cliff on the south-east side of Binnein Shuas, and three years later Doug Lang and Graeme Hunter made a systematic and energetic exploration of the whole crag, climbing 11 new routes in the course of two summers. Since then the south-east cliff of Binnein Shuas has become deservedly popular. Its sunny aspect and low altitude can often give enjoyable climbing when other higher crags are out of condition, and at the same time it has a true mountain atmosphere due to its remote situation facing the high mountains of Badenoch.

Of all the climbs on this cliff, one excels for its superb rock and magnificent situations – Ardverikie Wall. When Lang and Hunter made the first ascent in 1967 they predicted that this route would soon become a classic, and they were correct. Within a

92 *The approach to Binnein Shuas along the shore of Lochan na h-Earba*

93 *Ardverikie Wall from the head of Lochan na h-Earba*

year or two Ardverikie Wall was recognised as one of the best routes of Mild Severe standard in Scotland, and the best rock-climb in that vast tract of hills between Ben Nevis and the Cairngorms.

As one approaches the crag from the side of Lochan na h-Earba, the most obvious landmark is the big diagonal gully – Hidden Gully. On its left are the overhangs of the Fortress, on its right the vast smooth wall which forms the central and highest part of the cliff; it is there that Ardverikie Wall takes its direct line for 170 metres.

The start of the climb is at the lowest rocks right of Hidden Gully, and a short introductory pitch leads up by ledges to a recess among juniper bushes below a prominent overhang. The climb proper starts as one leaves the safety of the recess and steps out leftwards onto a very steep rib to climb by vertical cracks past the overhang. Then the angle eases slightly, but the pitch hardly relents for although the holds are good there are no resting places, and one just keeps on climbing in the hope of reaching a ledge before the rope runs out. Eventually the hoped-for ledge is reached, at the full extent of a 45 metre rope, and with it a superbly reassuring belay.

The next two pitches, both almost as long as the previous one, continue more or less directly up the

expanse of smooth slabs. The rock is pale grey granite, its rough surface sparkling with myriad crystals of quartz and mica. It is perfect rock for climbing, yet quite different from the granite of Arran or Glen Etive, for here on Ardverikie Wall there are plenty of holds, big and small, so that the steepness of the cliff belies the difficulty. Nothing, however, can detract from the feeling of exposure once one is high on the climb; even on the narrow belay ledges one is always aware of the space below.

At their top the slabs are barred by a small overlap, and the last problem of the climb is to surmount this. One can climb up a scoop until confronted by a short overhanging wall, and the step up this wall to reach easier rock is a fitting climax to the route, especially if one looks down just at the crucial move to savour the exposure. Beyond a grassy terrace there is another slab pitch, but it is easy by comparison with the climbing below.

Everyone reaching the top of Ardverikie Wall must surely agree with Doug Lang's description of this route as a classic. The only possible criticism might be that there is a lack of variety about its pitches; the character of the climbing is always the same. But such is that character – superbly steep and exposed climbing – that any such criticism would be churlish.

94 *The second pitch of Ardverikie Wall*

95 *The crux of Ardverikie Wall at the start of the fourth pitch*

20 The Traverse of Beinn a' Ghlo

Beinn a' Ghlo, the mountain of mist, stands on the south-western edge of the Grampians above Glen Garry. Its three rounded peaks rise conspicuously above the surrounding expanse of bare hills and moorland, and the graceful lines of its ridges and corries make it the most beautiful of the Grampian mountains.

Carn Liath (the grey hill, 975m) is the south-western peak, and from the south it appears like a simple cone rising in ever-steepening slopes above the upland farms in Glen Fender and Glen Girnaig. Five kilometres north-east the highest peak, Carn nan Gabhar (the hill of goats, 1121m) overlooks the tangle of remote hills and glens in the hinterland of Glen Tilt, and in between is the peak with one of the finest names in Scotland, Braigh Coire Chruinn-bhalgain (1070m); unfortunately its translation – the upland of the corrie of round little blisters – is distinctly less impressive.

Beinn a' Ghlo is very much a hill-walkers' mountain, in summer and winter. It is less well known as a skiers' mountain, but under winter snow it is just that, for then the smooth contours of its ridges, peaks and corries are ideal for skiing, and the traverse of the range from one end to the other and back again is a superb expedition.

The simplest approach is from Blair Atholl, up the Glen Fender road to Monzie farm as far as Loch Moraig, where one can start the traverse. If the road to Glen Girnaig is clear and permission is given, one can drive a few kilometres further, but the subsequent climb directly up Carn Liath, though short, is rather too steep for skis.

No easier introduction to any hill can be imagined

96 *The approach to Carn Liath across the moorland above Loch Moraig*

than the moorland which rises gradually from Loch Moraig towards Carn Liath. Mountain hares are everywhere, racing across the hillside at one's approach, and as the snows melt in spring, plovers and curlew return to their upland haunts to fill the air with their plaintive cries. The final climb to Carn Liath is steep, possibly too steep for skis if the snow is hard.

Now the hardest part of the day's climbing is done, and there is delightfully easy skiing along the broad crest of the ridge north-westwards to a shoulder of the hill, and then north-east to the first col; from the shoulder a descending traverse on the north-west side of the ridge takes one directly to the col in one long straight schuss. The continuation of the ridge northwards is easy, and one soon arrives at Braigh Coire Chruinn-bhalgain.

In clear weather there is no difficulty at all in following these ridges, but if Beinn a' Ghlo lives up to its name and mists shroud the mountain, then careful route-finding is needed. This is particularly

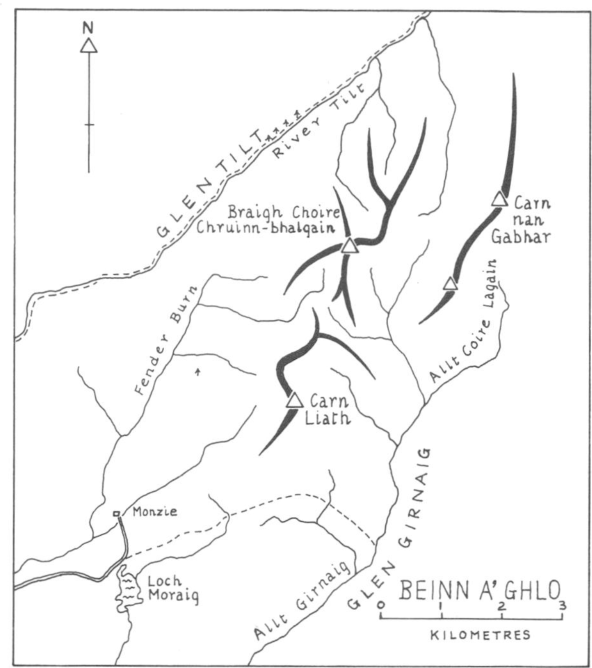

97 *Looking north-east from Carn Liath towards Braigh Coire Chruinn-bhalgain* (left) *and Carn nan Gabhar*

98 *Skiing south-west from Braigh Coire Chruinn-bhalgain towards Carn Liath*

true of the next section of the route which goes north-east to the edge of the hillside above the Bealach an Fhiodha. If one arrives at this edge too far south there may well be a cornice and a steep drop below, and one has to ski northwards to find easier ground for the descent to the bealach. From there a long ascending traverse north-eastwards leads to the highest point, Carn nan Gabhar, where two large cairns stand on the level summit ridge.

At this point one is nine kilometres as the crow flies (and a lot further as the skier goes) from Loch Moraig, and there is certainly a feeling of having come a long way. The return can be varied by skiing south from Carn nan Gabhar into Coire Lagain, a steep and exhilarating descent of 500 metres followed by a long level traverse round the foot of Carn Liath; a good snow-cover low down is needed for this route, otherwise there will be a lot of walking at the end of the day.

The alternative is to retrace one's tracks along the ridge; this is the better route if conditions are good, and there will be more than 1000 metres of excellent downhill skiing on the return to Loch Moraig. From the col north of Carn Liath it is worthwhile, if reserves of energy permit, making an ascending traverse to the shoulder of the hill high above the lonely Creag-choinnich Lodge to get into a good position for the last long run down the west face of Carn Liath. Given good conditions this is a superb descent, steep at first but becoming easier all the time, until finally one is gliding effortlessly across the snow-covered moor towards Loch Moraig.

21 Grampian Ski-Mountaineering

It sounds like heresy to suggest that some of Scotland's mountains may be rather dull, but even the most ardent hill-walker would be bound to admit that the vast expanse of featureless hills to the east of Drumochter Pass is a good deal less interesting than the mountains further north and west. These hills, the Eastern Grampians, stretch eastwards to Mount Keen and beyond, one rounded top after another, and with some notable exceptions (such as Beinn a' Ghlo, Lochnagar and Broad Cairn) they have few outstanding features. One could easily lose oneself in the utterly desolate country round the headwaters of the Tilt, the Geldie and the Feshie.

In winter however, under a covering of snow, there is a complete transformation; the brown and purple hills of summer become an undulating white wilderness, the rounded summits, broad ridges and shallow corries merging into a limitless snowscape. If anyone thinks that these hills lack character, let him go there in winter, for then he will find himself in country as wild and arctic as anything in Scotland, country that will test his fitness and mountain-craft, and even (if the blizzards come raging from the north) his powers of survival.

In winter the Eastern Grampians are superb hills for the cross-country ski-mountaineer. The many miles of smooth, easy-angled ridges and corries are ideal for langlauf skiing, and in the right conditions one can cover long distances using Nordic equipment, which would seem to be ideal for these hills.

There is no doubt that skis can transform a simple walk up and down a snow-covered hill into something much more interesting. The skier must study his mountain more carefully, noting its contours, humps and hollows to find the best lines of ascent and descent, and he must look for the snow-holding corries, the leeward sides of ridges where wind-blown snow has drifted and the snow-filled beds of streams which will take him far down into the glen at the end of the day. On the ascent there is the steady rhythm of climbing on skis which the walker cannot equal, a rhythm which may not make progress much quicker, but certainly makes it less tiring than walking in deep snow. Finally, coming downhill, there is the exhilaration of skiing virgin snow, an exhilaration which may also be challenging, for the quality of Scottish snow is infinitely varied; it is not unusual, as one skis down from mountain top to the glen, to

99 *Looking towards Glas Maol from Carn an Tuirc*

encounter in quick succession deep soft snow, breakable crust, spring snow and ice. Such variety is the spice of ski-mountaineering.

The road from Blairgowrie to Braemar crosses the Grampians by the Cairnwell pass at the head of Glen Shee, and the top of the pass, at an altitude of almost 700 metres, is a good starting point for ski tours to the east and west. Going eastwards, Glas Maol (1068m) can be quickly reached (particularly if the T-bars on Meall Odhar are used), and there one is at the edge of a plateau stretching north-eastwards for 12 kilometres to Lochnagar (1155m). The traverse from Glas Maol to Lochnagar is a superb expedition, skiing up and down across this vast undulating plateau over half a dozen intermediate swellings which Sir Hugh T. Munro rather generously classified as separate mountains: Cairn of Claise, Tom Buidhe, Tolmount, Cairn Bannoch, Carn an t-Sagairt Mor and Carn a' Choire Bhoidheach. This must, on a fine winter's day, be one of the pleasantest ways imaginable of collecting eight Munros.

On the other hand, when clouds come down on the mountains and blizzards rage, any expedition across this plateau in winter is likely to be a test of stamina and navigation skill, for there are few recognisable features, and even the summits are so flat that it may be difficult to find their cairns. To ski in blizzard and white-out conditions is difficult enough without having to navigate with pin-point accuracy at the same time, and one must also bear in mind that many of the descent routes from the plateau to Glen Isla, Glen Clova, Glen Callater and Glen Muick lie

101 *Langlauf across the level summits of the Grampians*

102 *The Eastern Grampian plateau. Looking south-west from Cairn of Claise towards Glas Maol and the cliffs at the head of the Caenlochan Glen*

down steep-walled corries where it is essential to find the right route if one is to avoid skiing over a cornice.

To the west of the Cairnwall pass the country is quite different, for on that side there is no continuous plateau but miles of rounded hills separated by deep glens. A very good tour can be made starting from The Cairnwell (933m), which can be reached by chair-lift, and skiing along the broad ridge, first north and then south-west and west to Carn a' Gheoidh (975m). The next point to aim for is Loch nan Eun, five kilometres distant to the north-west, and there is a good run down to the Baddach Burn before crossing the very featureless hill, Carn a' Chlarsaich, to reach it.

Once at Loch nan Eun at about 800 metres there is a choice of routes, for one is at the centre of several hills, all eminently skiable. The highest of these hills to the north and west of the loch is Beinn Iutharn Mhor (1045m), and it can be climbed before returning southwards to Glas Tulaichean (1051m). The climb up this peak goes along the edge of its two eastern corries, the most interesting features of the mountain, and the ski run from the summit down the broad and smooth south-east ridge is delightfully easy. Eventually, depending on the snow-line, the best descent is likely to be down the corrie above Glenlochsie Lodge, and unless there is snow right down in the glen the day will end with six kilometres on foot back to the Spittal of Glenshee. It is at this time, when skis are no longer gliding across the snow but weighing heavily on one's shoulders, that the truth of that saying about pleasure and pain becomes very real.

22 Lochnagar Granite and Ice

It was Dr. J.H.B. Bell, one of the greatest of Scottish mountaineers, who is quoted as saying: 'Any fool can climb good rock, but it takes craft and cunning to get up vegetatious schist and granite.' It is not known if he had Lochnagar in mind when he said this, but it could have been so for he was well acquainted with the mountain and its granite cliffs, which have more than their fair share of loose rock and vegetation clinging to every available ledge and crack. Climbs with names such as The Crumbling Cranny, Grovel Wall and The Gutter speak for themselves. Notwithstanding this, Dr. Bell's remark has been taken by Aberdonian climbers as an almost divine pronouncement of the superiority of the granite mountains of the north-east, among which Lochnagar is pre-eminent, and of themselves as being particularly gifted with the necessary craft and cunning to climb them by the most difficult routes. Needless to say, these opinions are not shared by other Scottish climbers.

The greatest of J.H.B. Bell's achievements on Lochnagar was his ascent of Eagle Ridge with Nancy Forsyth in 1941. Five years earlier he had reconnoitred the ridge and reached the summit plateau by a route on the flank now known as Eagle Buttress. In 1940 W.S. Scroggie and J.G. Ferguson straightened out the earlier route, but failed to complete a direct ascent of the ridge. This was accomplished by Bell in the following year, and so in the summer of 1941 when climbing in Scotland (as elsewhere in Europe) was at its lowest ebb, two superb granite ridges were finally overcome after repeated attempts – the South Ridge of the Rosa Pinnacle and Eagle Ridge.

The north-east corrie of Lochnagar is formed by a crescent of cliffs towering above the dark lochan of the same name. These crags, 'the steep frowning glories' of Byron's familiar verse, are a succession of buttresses and gullies about 200 metres high. Eagle Ridge can be recognised as the rather slender butt-

103 *Lochnagar, its north-eastern corrie and loch*

ress near the east end of the cirque; on its left is the deep corridor of the Douglas-Gibson Gully in which winter snow lingers until mid-summer, and on its right is the shallow depression of Parallel Gully A. The base of the ridge is broad and slabby, but higher up it narrows to form a succession of vertical steps and knife-edge crests.

The climb starts just above the foot of the ridge on the Douglas-Gibson Gully side where a prominent right-angled groove cuts into the flank of the ridge. Often in early summer there is a mini-bergschrund to be crossed to get onto the rocks, and the groove itself is a good pitch, harder than it looks until good holds are reached near the top, and it is a salutary warning that Eagle Ridge is a climb to be taken seriously. Easier climbing leads rightwards across the ridge, up slabs and cracks and finally back to the crest at a small exposed platform, but these first few pitches are little more than a preliminary skirmish before the serious stuff ahead. Above the platform the ridge, now narrow and exposed, rears up abruptly for 20 metres; this is the First Tower. The climbing is Severe, but the granite is perfect (no vegetation here); first an awkward move up into a corner on the right, then another short traverse right, up with difficulty, back left onto the exposed crest and a strenuous pull-up to reach a welcome haven in a sentry-box. Altogether a superb pitch.

More relaxed climbing follows up an easy-angled slab and a short wall to a platform on the crest from which a narrow ledge leads rightwards. From the end of this ledge one climbs a steep crack for a few

104 *The Lochnagar cliffs. Eagle Ridge on the left, Raeburn's Gully on the right*

105 *The first pitch of Eagle Ridge*

metres to regain the crest of the ridge where it forms a knife-edge abutting against a short wall. This wall, split by an open crack, is generally regarded as the crux of the climb; certainly Bell considered it to be the crux on his first ascent, and he like everyone else who reaches this point was greatly impressed by the exposure of the situation, for the east side of the ridge falls sheer into the Douglas-Gibson Gully. The difficulty, however, is short-lived, and two or three moves on awkward sloping holds bring good handholds into reach.

The plateau is now close at hand, but there is at least one more pitch which is full of interesting moves if one keeps close to the crest. The granite of Eagle Ridge provides an endless variety of intriguing little climbing problems right to the top. No wonder that Bell considered it to be unique among the long precipitous mountain ridges in Britain. That is an opinion which all would endorse.

Snow and ice give added character and grandeur to Lochnagar, and the mountain gives the best winter climbing in the north-east; every ridge, buttress and gully has its route, and every route is one of the finest of its kind in Scotland. There is, too, the advantage that the corrie, unlike many of the remote Cairngorm corries, is accessible even on a short winter day. The vegetation which detracts from summer climbing is no problem when masked by snow and ice, and there may even by times when its presence is a positive advantage, for if snow and ice are lacking at some crucial point on a climb it is often possible to cut excellent holds in hard-frozen turf. It may not be very aesthetic, but it can be very reassuring.

Prior to 1949 winter climbs on Lochnagar were few in number; the easy and medium standard gullies had been climbed, but little else. The impetus came from Bill Brooker with his winter ascent of Shadow Buttress A at the end of that year, and he was soon followed by Tom Patey and other members of the very active Aberdeen climbing teams of the 1950s. No summer route was considered too hard for a winter attempt, and many such as Eagle Ridge and its neighbouring Parallel Buttress produced quite exceptional climbs which still, 20 years later, are considered to be in the highest class of Scottish winter climbs.

Lochnagar in winter is not, however, a mountain for experts only. There are gullies of every standard

106 *The Whaleback pitch above the First Tower on Eagle Ridge*

107 *The crux pitch on Eagle Ridge; the hard move is up the crack just beyond the climber*

108 *The Lochnagar corrie in winter*

109 *The summit cliffs of Lochnagar*

to give climbing for everyone, with the warning that most of these gullies acquire huge cornices during the winter, and when the spring thaws come impressive avalanches trundle down them as the cornices collapse. At the lower end of the scale there is the Black Spout, the winter trade route from the corrie to the summit. There is, inevitably, Raeburn's Gully, for the old master seems to have a route in nearly every Scottish corrie, and on Lochnagar his gully is possibly the most popular winter route; its difficulty diminishes as the season progresses, the big pitch becoming banked by snow and the grade dropping from III to II. Going up the scale, Parallel Gully A, Pinnacle Gully One and Giant's Head Chimney are progressively more difficult and at the top of the list Parallel Gully B, Polyphemus Gully and Douglas-Gibson Gully are formidable climbs.

Douglas-Gibson Gully, and in particular its vertical 60 metre headwall, acquired a reputation for extreme difficulty following the failure of Messrs Douglas and Gibson to climb it, and even the solo first ascent by C. Ludwig in 1933 did nothing to dispel this reputation. When Tom Patey made the first winter ascent with G.B. Leslie in 1950 he launched himself on the meteoric climbing career that took him all over Scotland and abroad to the Greater Ranges. However, after many mountain adventures, his feelings for Lochnagar could still be summarised in his characteristic verse:

'Masherbrum, Gasherbrum, Distegil Sar;
Make excellent training for Dark Lochnagar.'

110 *Raeburn's Gully, Lochnagar*

23 The Mitre Ridge of Beinn a' Bhuird

Beyond Glen Derry the eastern Cairngorms are dominated by the two great plateau mountains Beinn a' Bhuird and Ben Avon. Seen from Braemar, Ben Avon looks the more interesting of the two, with its many granite tors like warts on the summit plateau. Beinn a' Bhuird to its west looks rather flat and uninteresting, well deserving its name, which means the table hill.

But anyone who judges the Cairngorms by distant views is likely to form a very wrong impression. Only when one penetrates far into the glens and reaches the high and remote corries can the real character of these mountains be fully appreciated. This is as true of Beinn a' Bhuird (1196m) as of any of the Cairngorms, for high on its eastern and northern sides are hidden some of the finest corries of the range.

One of the features which distinguish climbing in the Cairngorms from climbing elsewhere in Scotland (in Glencoe for example) is the long approach march which usually precedes a day's climbing. Undoubtedly it is these long marches to and from the distant corries, by day and by night, in summer and winter, that have given Cairngorm

111 *The Mitre Ridge. Two climbers are roping up on the edge of the snow patch below the first pitch*

112 *The first pitch of Mitre Ridge*

climbers their reputation for toughness; they think nothing of a 15 kilometre walk to a high camp or a bivouac under a boulder as a prelude to their day's climbing.

The approach to Beinn a' Bhuird from Deeside is certainly long, but by no means tedious. On the one hand there is the walk up Glen Quoich from Allanaquoich through the pinewoods of the Caledonian Forest. To wander among these ancient forests, whose Scots Pines seem to be almost as enduring as the hills above them, is one of the great joys of climbing in the Cairngorms. The alternative approach by the Slugain Glen is quite different in character; the pinewoods of Deeside are left behind soon after passing Alltdourie, and one enters the narrow Gleann an t-Slugain, where birch trees cling to the steep hillside above the stream. Higher up, the path meanders through the Fairy Glen among little grassy meadows and stunted birches to reach the ruins of Slugain Lodge.

These two approaches converge along the head-waters of the Quoich Water, and Beinn a' Bhuird begins to reveal itself. High above the glen the rocky point of A'Chioch separates Coire na Ciche from Coire an Dubh Lochan; the latter corrie, which one can barely glimpse from below, is one of the most

113 *Bell's Route on the Second Tower of Mitre Ridge*

114 *The upper part of Mitre Ridge from the west*

beautiful in the Cairngorms. Our path, however, heads due north to the Sneck, the col between Beinn a' Bhuird and Ben Avon, and here one enters the Garbh Choire by a downward traverse across steep gravelly slopes.

The Garbh Choire is ringed by buttresses and gullies, but one's eye is drawn immediately to the great central feature of the corrie, the soaring ridge which dwarfs everything else. This is the Mitre Ridge. It is not only the height and isolation of the Mitre Ridge that make such an impression, but also its splendid features – the broad base of overlapping slabs, the steepening buttress above and the final pinnacled ridge leading to the plateau 200 metres above the foot. Its challenge is obvious.

When, one day in July 1933, Sandy Wedderburn and his companions climbed the Mitre Ridge by two ways, the Direct Route and the West Face, a high-water-mark was reached in Cairngorm climbing that was not to be equalled for another eight years – when J.H.B. Bell climbed Eagle Ridge on Lochnagar to produce a route of equal character.

The Direct Route starts a few paces right of the foot of the ridge, following the corner between a long slab and the vertical wall on its left. This first pitch, the longest and hardest of the climb, is a continuous struggle upwards, the left foot jamming in the corner while the right foot searches for every available wrinkle on the slab, and occasional handholds on the left wall help progress. The slab ends below a short overhanging wall, the sting in the tail of this pitch, and one has to summon reserves of energy to grasp the jughandle holds high on the left wall and pull up to a resting place.

After the superb climbing of the first pitch, the next 60 metres are something of an anticlimax, as one climbs easily up a rake leading round the west side of the ridge to reach the foot of a short dark chimney. This pitch goes easily enough, provided one avoids too deep an involvement in the innermost recesses of the chimney, and above it the leader must tread carefully as he scrambles up a little gully to avoid bombarding the rest of his team with gravel or even heavier debris.

At the top of this gully one emerges onto the crest of the ridge, now narrow and exposed, and the climb continues up this crest on perfect steep granite to a ledge below the First Tower. Now the way ahead lies up a five metre corner where a perfect layback crack and an equally perfect spike for a running belay give the most delightful pitch of the climb, ending in a grassy corner. Here the team can relax in comfort while the leader climbs steeply to the airy tip of the First Tower.

From this tower one looks across a little gap to the Second Tower. Its outer face seems impregnable, and the original route goes round to the left, but the best route without doubt is Bell's Variation. Crossing the gap, the outer face of the tower is climbed for a few metres until it is possible to traverse right, round a corner onto the west face. Suddenly there is a feeling of exposure, for the whole height of the west face of Mitre Ridge is below one's heels; but the climb goes without difficulty up a steep little groove until one is standing on the pedestal at its top. The wall ahead is vertical and holdless, but a step leftwards and a long reach for a hidden handhold solve all problems, and a glorious pull-up over space lands one on the Second Tower.

Now the difficulties of Mitre Ridge are past, and one scrambles along a narrow ridge, over three little pinnacles to the last short step leading to the grassy expanse of Beinn a' Bhuird's plateau. Not far away a little stream flows down from Cnap a' Chleirich to tumble into the Garbh Choire, an invitation to relax and slake one's thirst. However, the temptation to linger must be tempered by the thought that there is a long way to go on the return journey to the pine-woods of Alltdourie or the Quoich.

24 The Cairngorms on Ski

Among the mountains of Scotland the Cairngorms have a character that is unique. The height and scale of these mountains, the vast featureless plateaux that form their highest tops and the long glens which penetrate into their heart from the valleys of the Dee and Spey give them a feeling of size and remoteness that is unequalled elsewhere in Scotland.

The whole character of the Cairngorms, from the surrounding forests up to the summits, is more akin to the arctic wilderness than to the rest of Scotland. The arctic-alpine vegetation has a richness and variety not matched elsewhere in this country, the high plateaux are frequented by several species of birds whose home is more commonly in the arctic, and last but not least the weather of the Cairngorms has an arctic quality which is seldom equalled in other parts of Scotland. When the winds blow from the north laden with snow, the blizzards which sweep across the Cairngorms have a savage fury. It is this combination of the height and scale of the mountains and the arctic storms which can rage at any time of the year that makes the Cairngorms so demanding of respect, and the history of climbing and walking in these mountains records many tragedies caused by the blizzards of winter and spring.

On the other hand, when the storms abate the Cairngorms take on a much more benign character, and in such conditions to walk or ski across the mountains and to explore and climb in the corries are rewarding experiences for the solitude and quiet of these remote places.

With their vast flat-topped summits and long winters of snow cover (often from November to May) the Cairngorms are ideal for ski-mountaineering. The earliest recorded expedition on skis was in 1913 when a party skied from Aviemore to Deeside over Cairngorm and Ben Macdhui. In the following years ski-mountaineers, few in number but dedicated nevertheless, made ascents on ski of nearly every major peak in the Cairngorms. In 1953 Norman Clark traversed the

115 *Skiing off the summit of Cairngorm at the start of the Four Peaks Traverse*

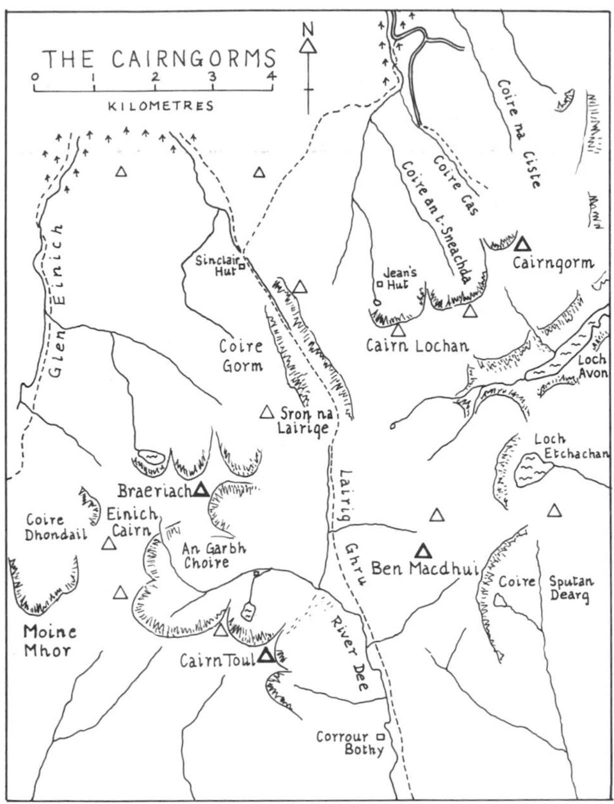

four highest tops, and in 1962 Adam Watson made the longest single-day traverse yet recorded when he crossed Ben Avon and the five highest Cairngorms, a total distance of 61 kilometres. Now the downhill skiing developments in Coire Cas and Coire na Ciste on Cairngorm attract hundreds of skiers, and an increasing number of them, possibly urged to escape from these two overcrowded corries, are taking to the plateaux and high tops on their skis.

Among ski-mountaineers there is always debate as to the best type of equipment for their sport. There are those who favour light Scandinavian skis with their flexible bindings, and there is no doubt that for the gently undulating Cairngorm plateaux in conditions of soft snow this type of ski is ideal. On the other hand there are those who point to the unpredictability of Scottish snow conditions, the frequency of hard icy conditions and the advantages of conventional downhill skis with steel edges and rigid bindings both for these conditions and for steep downhill skiing. These skis are certainly better suited to deal with the great variety of Scottish snow conditions and terrain, but they cannot match the Scandinavian skis on easy ground and soft snow.

There is an almost limitless choice of ski-tours across and around the Cairngorms, and anyone poring over a map will discover many possibilities for himself. Naturally the highest tops have the greatest attraction, and usually the best snow cover, so it is not surprising that the traverse of the four highest – Cairngorm, Ben Macdui (formerly spelt Ben Macdhui, as on the map), Cairn Toul and Braeriach – is held by many to be the best ski-tour in these mountains.

Cairngorm (1245m) is the usual starting point, for one can use the lift system and reach its summit with little effort. The traverse starts with a short run westwards and then the gradual climb and descent round the edge of Coire an t-Sneachda to the col below Cairn Lochan. Now one can head southwards across the undulating plateau towards Ben Macdui (1309m), four kilometres distant. So featureless is this plateau that in bad visibility pin-point compass navigation is essential, for there are no landmarks until the cairn of Ben Macdui is reached.

Now comes one of the highlights of the traverse – the ski-run from Ben Macdui down to the Lairig Ghru. There are two superb descents: south and then south-westwards by the Allt Clach nan Taillear (the Tailors' Burn), or north-west and then west down the Allt a' Choire Mhoir. Both routes must be among the best off-piste ski-runs in Scotland; the former is longer (the descent is about 700 metres), but the latter is steeper and more exhilarating and has the advantage of finishing higher in the Lairig, thus leaving less climbing on the other side. If Cairn Toul (1293m) is the next objective, then the Tailors' Burn is the logical route, but there is the prospect of wading across the River Dee if one is to avoid the long detour downstream to the bridge at Corrour Bothy.

The ascent to Cairn Toul is a long grind, possibly following the snow-filled hollow of the burn flowing from Coire an t-Saighdeir. The angle is as steep as is comfortable for uphill climbing on skins, and it is a relief to reach the more level corrie and traverse north into Coire an t-Sabhail and finish the climb up one of its bounding ridges.

From Cairn Toul there is a splendid undulating traverse of five kilometres round the edge of An Garbh Choire over Sgor an Lochain Uaine (also known as the Angel's Peak) and the South-West Top of Braeriach to Braeriach itself (1296m). An Garbh Choire is the finest and remotest of all the Cairngorm corries, the true heart of these mountains. It is not a single corrie, but a huge amphitheatre enclosing four lesser corries, and an almost continuous line of cliffs, heavily corniced in winter

116 *Perfect spring snow on the run from Ben Macdui down the Allt a' Choire Mhoir to the Lairig Ghru*

117 *Looking south from Braeriach to Cairn Toul*

118 *Braeriach from Loch Pityoulish*

and spring and holding snow throughout the year in its innermost recesses, marks the edge of the plateau extending from Cairn Toul to Braeriach. In good conditions this is a delightful langlauf, but in bad weather it may need careful navigation, keeping close but not too close to the corniced edge.

From Braeriach the best return to one's starting point at Cairngorm is eastwards and then north over Sron na Lairige and down Coire Gorm. This is another superb corrie for carefree skiing; the angle is easy and there is a glorious descent of 450 metres in two kilometres, to the point where one has to traverse eastwards through a little gap to reach the Sinclair Memorial Hut in the Lairig Ghru. From there the return through the Chalamain Gap to the foot of Coire Cas is either easy level skiing or tedious walking – depending on how low the snow is lying.

It is always more satisfying to make a true traverse, finishing the day on the far side of the mountains from one's starting point. Thus a better end to the day can be made by skiing from Braeriach to Glen Feshie. On the map this looks a lot longer than the return to Coire Cas, but this is not necessarily so. The first five kilometres take one south-westwards from Braeriach past the Einich Cairn and in a long easy run down onto the Moine Mhor – the great moss which lies between the Glen Feshie hills and Cairn Toul. Passing Lochan nan Cnapan at the lowest point of the moss, one climbs gradually for two and a half kilometres to Carn Ban Mor (1052m), a flat and featureless hill overlooking Glen Feshie. Finally, there is pleasant skiing either down Coire Ruadh or directly towards Achlean farm.

Taken this way, the traverse of the four highest Cairngorms becomes the finest day's high-level skiing in Scotland that is within the capability of ordinary mortals. It deserves a fine day in late April or May, for then the days are long enough to complete the route comfortably and the spring snow may well be at its best.

25 The Northern Corries of Cairngorm

It is not so many years since the present-day highway from Aviemore to Loch Morlich was little more than a narrow gravel road, and beyond Glenmore Lodge only a footpath led up through the forest towards Cairngorm; Coire Cas was an empty, silent and rather characterless corrie in which ptarmigan lived undisturbed. Changes began to happen about 1946 when Lord Malcolm Douglas Hamilton started the climbing courses at Aviemore which led a year or two later to the establishment of Glenmore Lodge as Scotland's first (and for many years only) centre for mountain training. Skiing soon followed, and within a few years the first pistes were being beaten down in Coire Cas by ever-increasing numbers of skiers.

In those early days the Glenmore Lodge staff included many dedicated amateurs, and under their enthusiastic guidance hundreds of climbers tackled their first rock-climb on the little crags of Creag a' Chalamain and cut their first steps in the snows of Coire an t-Sneachda or Coire an Lochain – the northern corries of Cairngorm. By the end of a week's course promising students might graduate to the damp, dark recesses of Savage Slit or the narrow icy

119 *Coire an t-Sneachda*

Vent, two climbs on Cairn Lochan which in those days had quite a reputation for difficulty.

Now the new Glenmore Lodge is staffed by dedicated professionals, but still the first steps in winter climbing for many are taken in the same two corries, though the ancient art of step-cutting tends nowadays to be quickly superseded by more modern techniques with crampons and short axes. Many of the recent advances in winter climbing techniques have been pioneered by Bill March and John Cunningham at Glenmore Lodge, and these advances have put Scottish ice-climbing in the forefront to such an extent that there seem to be climbers (many of them from North America) who are prepared to travel thousands of miles at the uncertain prospect of finding freezing conditions and good ice in Scottish gullies.

The northern corries are not by any means the preserve of Glenmore Lodge climbers. In the 1930s founder members of the newly formed Moray Mountaineering Club made several first ascents there in summer and winter, and it is safe to say that in the last 30 years more climbers have taken their first steps in winter climbing in these corries than anywhere else in Scotland. This popularity is not surprising; there are snow and ice climbs of all standards of difficulty which are short and not too serious, and the corries are (since the building of the road to Coire Cas) the most accessible in the Cairngorms, which is important on a short winter day. Last, but possibly not least, the night-life of Aviemore has no equal in any other Scottish mountain centre; the days are long since past when climbers spent the long winter evenings huddled in their tents by the shore of Loch Morlich.

Coire an t-Sneachda is rather an open corrie, and there is no feeling of being hemmed in by beetling cliffs as one stands at the lochan. The ribs and gullies which sweep up to the plateau are not very steep, and most of the climbs in the corrie are quite easy. Between Alladin's Buttress in the centre of the corrie and Fluted Buttress to the right are the narrow Trident gullies in which the only possible problems may be big cornices. Spiral Gully (II) diverges right from the foot of the Trident and is usually not corniced, so that it may be an easier proposition when cornices are big. A short distance further right Broken Gully (III) is the hardest of the gullies, lying to the left side of Fingers Ridge, the well-defined

120 *A long stride at the top of Fingers Ridge, Coire an t-Sneachda*

121 *The cliffs of Coire an Lochain, at whose foot a big bergschrund has opened up in late spring*

122 *Coire an Lochain in spring, showing the formation of Scotland's only glacier*

ridge leading up to two prominent little pinnacles on the skyline. This ridge has also been climbed in winter (IV) and is an enjoyable route.

Coire an Lochain is altogether a more impressive corrie; four dark buttresses rise above a huge granite slab which in winter becomes a uniform snow slope of about 40 degrees. Between the buttresses there are well-defined gullies each about 100 metres high: on the left the narrow Vent with its single ice-pitch (II–III), in the centre the easy slanting Couloir (I) and on the right Y Gully. The left branch of Y Gully is short and steep (III); the right branch is easier (II), but the angle increases all the way up to the cornice and in conditions of soft snow the final part of the climb may be dangerous. There are other excellent winter routes on the buttresses, generally harder than the gullies: the grooves to the right of The Vent for example, or No. 3 Buttress which is the bounding ridge of The Couloir, or (possibly finest of all) Savage Slit, the very deep chimney which cleaves the face of West Buttress. Without doubt there is in this fine little corrie a great variety of short winter climbs of all grades.

Beware however, for Coire an Lochain also has an evil reputation for avalanches. Snow lying on the huge slab in the centre of the corrie is liable to slide down, particularly in thaw conditions when melt-water trickling down the slab releases the overlying snow. The resulting avalanches can be quite spectacular, sending huge masses of snow and ice crashing into the lochan far below. Occasionally in spring a small glacier forms in the corrie; snow many metres thick lying on the slab starts to slip down, possibly for only a short distance, leaving a bergschrund below the upper cliffs, forming crevasses lower down and an ice-wall at the front of the sliding snow. This formation of a small glacier is unique in Scotland, but it does give some impression of how our mountains might look if they were just a few hundred metres higher.

26 The Rough Bounds of Knoydart

The way from Fort William westwards to Mallaig is the Road to the Isles, and on its north side the country is a tangle of remote glens and rugged mountains, with the long sea-lochs of Nevis and Hourn biting deeply into this, the roughest part of the Western Highlands. These are the districts of Knoydart, Morar and the western part of Lochaber, and of these it is Knoydart that holds the greatest attraction for climbers, for there on the south side of Loch Hourn and round the head of Loch Nevis the mountains are highest, steepest and most rugged. Not for nothing is this region known as the Rough Bounds of Knoydart.

It is impossible to dissociate the wild Knoydart hills from the wanderings of Prince Charles Edward Stuart after the Battle of Culloden in 1746. The Prince's flight from Hanoverian troops took him through Knoydart and Morar not once but three times as he eluded his pursuers that summer. These hills and corries may have been ideal to cover his flight, but he spent many miserable days and nights among them, hiding in the heather and under boulders, sometimes sweltering in the sun and plagued by midges, and at other times lashed by rain and soaked to the skin.

Knoydart is first and foremost hill-walkers'

123 *On the Ridge from Garbh Chioch Mhor to Sgurr na Ciche*

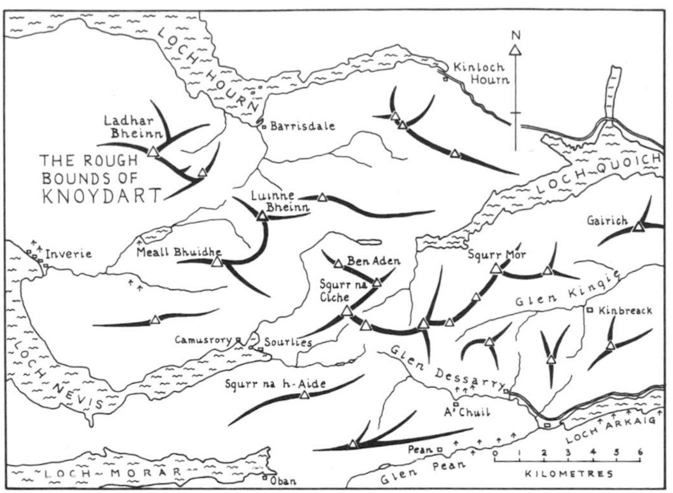

country, for although the mountains are steep and rocky there has been little rock-climbing recorded on them. Certainly in Coire Dhorrcail of Ladhar Bheinn there are buttresses and gullies over 300 metres high, but they are so vegetatious that the only worthwhile climbs that have been done on them have been in winter conditions. For adventurous hill-walkers, however, there is the opportunity to get right off the beaten track into true wilderness country, miles from the nearest signs of civilisation. One should take a map but not a guidebook, for guidebooks tend to inhibit initiative, and the pleasures of Knoydart are those of exploration and discovery, of striking out westwards from the head of Loch Arkaig through narrow passes to reach the remotest corners of this region.

Sgurr na Ciche (1040m) is the highest mountain of Knoydart, standing like a beacon above a turbulent sea of lesser peaks. From it a rough ridge goes eastwards over Garbh Chioch Mhor towards Sgurr nan Coireachan (953m), the most remarkable feature of this ridge being the stone dike which runs for two or three kilometres along its crest. Years ago men must have laboured long and hard to build this wall, presumably to prevent the sheep of Kinlochquoich from straying into Glen Dessarry, or vice-versa. Far below this ridge on its south side the Mam na Cloich Airde is the pass from Glen Dessary westwards into Knoydart; it is a place of silent beauty, with its two lochans nestling below steep crags and the stream winding through the narrow glen.

Further north-west Ladhar Bheinn (1020m), Luinne Bheinn (939m) and Meall Buidhe (946m) are the three high mountains between Loch Hourn and Loch Nevis. Of these Ladhar Bheinn is the finest, its grandest feature being Coire Dhorrcail on the north-east side of the mountain. This corrie is enclosed by the subsidiary peaks of Stob a' Chearcaill on the east and Stob a' Choire Odhair on the west, and the circuit of the corrie over the three peaks, which can easily be done from Barrisdale, is the best traverse of the mountain. Anyone lucky enough to find good snow conditions on Ladhar Bheinn should make the most of a rare opportunity and tackle one of the winter routes such as Viking Gully in the headwall of Coire Dhorrcail, or Gaberlunzie Gully in the centre of Stob a' Chearcaill's north-west face. Both these routes, of Grade III/IV standard, were climbed by Tom Patey and his companions in unusually favourable conditions in April 1962. However, the remoteness of Ladhar Bheinn and its mild west coast climate have discouraged climbers in winter, and only a handful of new routes have been done in more recent years.

There are half a dozen bothies in and around Knoydart which are a great asset to anyone climbing and walking in the area. These remote cottages, once the homes of shepherds and keepers but long since deserted, have been renovated by dedicated climbers and bothy dwellers, and with the consent of landowners are now available to give simple shelter to wanderers through the hills. Often the shelter is no more than four walls, a roof and a dry floor, but it is better than a tent when the rains come, and going from bothy to bothy one can travel lightly laden across the length and breadth of Knoydart, from Oban on Loch Morar to Kinbreack in Glen Kingie, and from Pean to Sourlies at the head of Loch Nevis.

Finally, no description of Knoydart would be complete (or honest) without mention of the fact that it is right in the area of Scotland's highest rainfall – over four metres per year. This makes the bothies doubly welcome when the deluges come and also introduces an added potential hazard, namely river-crossing. It may be impossible to cross some of the turbulent streams after two or three days' heavy rain, and one could well find oneself almost trapped at Sourlies, unable to get out except by climbing high up into the hills. In conditions such as these it would be more apt to describe the Rough Bounds as being the land of the mountain and the flood.

124 *The west end of Loch Arkaig, looking towards Sgurr Thuilm*
125 *Sourlies Bothy at the head of Loch Nevis*
126 *Ben Aden and Sgurr na Ciche from Camusrory at the head of Loch Nevis*

27 Kintail Ridges

The topography of the Western Highlands has a remarkably well defined pattern; to the west of the Great Glen there is a succession of glens running east to west, and between them serried ranks of mountains form parallel ridges many kilometres long. Nowhere is this structure better seen than in Glen Shiel, which is enclosed by high ridges on both sides along its whole length, from the watershed near Cluanie Inn to Loch Duich. On the north side of the glen the finest peaks of a 14 kilometre ridge are the Five Sisters of Kintail. On the other side the South Cluanie Ridge begins at Creag a' Mhaim and extends westwards over peak after peak, culminating 17 kilometres away on The Saddle, the highest mountain on the south side of the glen.

The Five Sisters are, in appearance at least, the best known mountains of the Western Highlands. At the north-west end of the group the peaks which overlook the head of Loch Duich have a beautiful symmetry of shape which is well seen from the loch-side near Ratagan. The western sides of Sgurr Fhuaran and its neighbours tower above Glen Shiel in 1000 metres of steep grassy slopes scarred by deep ravines. In contrast, the seldom visited north-east side of the range is a series of wild corries, sanctuaries for red deer and mountain goats.

The traverse of the Five Sisters is a classic hill-walk; splendid peaks, splendid views on a clear day and few difficulties in route-finding when the weather is not clear, for there is a tenuous path nearly all the way. Surprisingly for a ridge with such distinctive peaks, only the two highest Sisters count as Munros, the others being lesser heights. The easiest starting point for the traverse is in Glen Shiel, directly below the Bealach an Lapain; there is a wide gap in the forest at this point, and the ascent of the grassy hillside is steep and unrelenting. It is short, however, and an hour is enough to reach the bealach at the south-east end of the Five Sisters.

Now the ridge walk proper begins along the

narrow grassy crest, rising gradually to Sgurr nan Spainteach and continuing over a few minor tops to Sgurr na Ciste Duibhe (1027m). Just before reaching this peak one passes a curious rocky hollow on the crest of the ridge which might be a bit confusing to anyone descending eastwards in thick mist. The ridge over Sgurr na Carnach is broad and there is a rather long steep climb to reach Sgurr Fhuaran (1068m), the highest of the Glen Shiel mountains.

Continuing northwards the ridge becomes narrower again as one approaches Sgurr nan Saighead. This peak looks the most impressive of the Five Sisters, for its summit is sharp pointed and its north-east face is a succession of steep slabby ribs and gullies plunging down to Gleann Lichd. There is the possibility of some good winter climbing here, but the rock seems quite unsuitable for any serious summer climbing.

The last of the Five Sisters is Sgurr na Moraich (876m), but it is probably the least often climbed, for it is all too easy to avoid it at the end of the day and take the direct descent to Loch Duich down the Allt a' Chruinn.

On the other side of Glen Shiel The Saddle is the supreme mountain. Its summit is the meeting point of three ridges whose steep sides plunge down to deep ice-worn corries, and it is up these ridges and corries that the usual routes from Glen Shiel lie. The south-west side of The Saddle rises above the remote and beautiful head of Glen Arnisdale, but this corner of the mountain is seldom visited.

The main crest of The Saddle is a narrow ridge running west to east from Spidean Dhomhuill Bhric (940m) over the summit (1010m) to Sgurr nan Forcan and beyond towards Glen Shiel. A subsidiary ridge goes north from the summit to Sgurr na Creige, and on its west side is the impressive Coire Uaine with the loch of the same name nestling in its deep hollow. For the climber, however, the finest feature of The Saddle is the east ridge of Sgurr nan Forcan – the Forcan Ridge – a rocky, knife-edge crest broken into little pinnacles. This ridge is the highlight of The Saddle and a route which everyone should savour.

About five kilometres up Glen Shiel from Shiel Bridge a stalkers' path starts at the roadside and climbs across the hillside south-west of the glen. One follows this path to its end and continues south-

127 *The peak of Sgurr nan Saighead in the Five Sisters*

128 *The lower peak at the north end of the Five Sisters ridge*

THE KINTAIL MOUNTAINS
The Saddle and the Five Sisters.

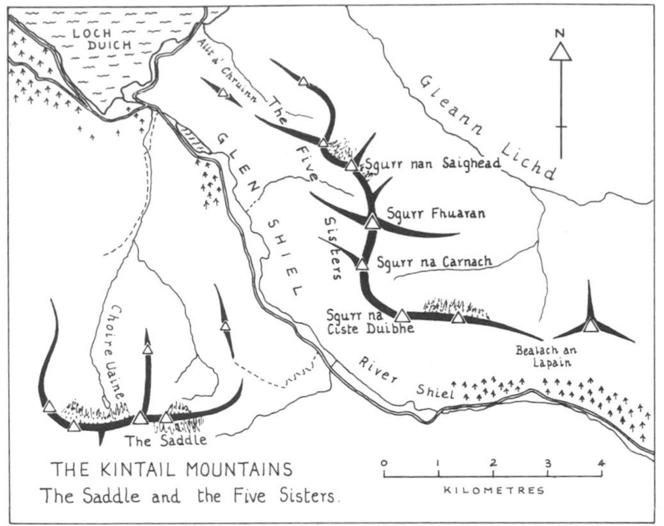

westwards along a broad ridge towards Sgurr nan Forcan. Once the rocky Forcan Ridge is reached the best scrambling is had by staying right on the crest, climbing every little obstacle directly and enjoying the exposure of this narrow ridge. There are, however, no difficulties that cannot be avoided, and this delightful scramble ends all too soon on the summit of Sgurr nan Forcan. Now the main top of The Saddle appears, rising boldly to the west and looking still a long way off, though it is less than a kilometre away as the crow flies.

From Sgurr nan Forcan one descends steeply at first and there is an easy pitch with good holds; otherwise the ridge, though narrow, is perfectly straightforward and leads over an intermediate hump to The Saddle. Continuing westwards, the most impressive feature of the walk towards Spidean Dhomhuill Bhric is the very steep drop on the Coire Uaine side of the ridge which gives a feeling of exposure. The Spidean is a fine peak, with a steep spur dropping north-eastwards into the corrie which makes an interesting route of ascent. The usual traverse goes over Sgurr Leac nan Each and northwards down a broad grassy ridge.

Now, with only a long and easy descent to Shiel Bridge ahead, one can appreciate the wonderful view towards the west where the bold outline of Beinn Sgritheall dominates. Further south Ladhar Bheinn rises grandly across the deep trough of Loch Hourn, and between these two mountains, far beyond the Sound of Sleat, the Cuillin of Rum seem to float on the horizon. It is a view to remember long after one has left the ridge and dropped down into the deep glen of Coire Uaine.

129 *The Forcan Ridge of The Saddle*

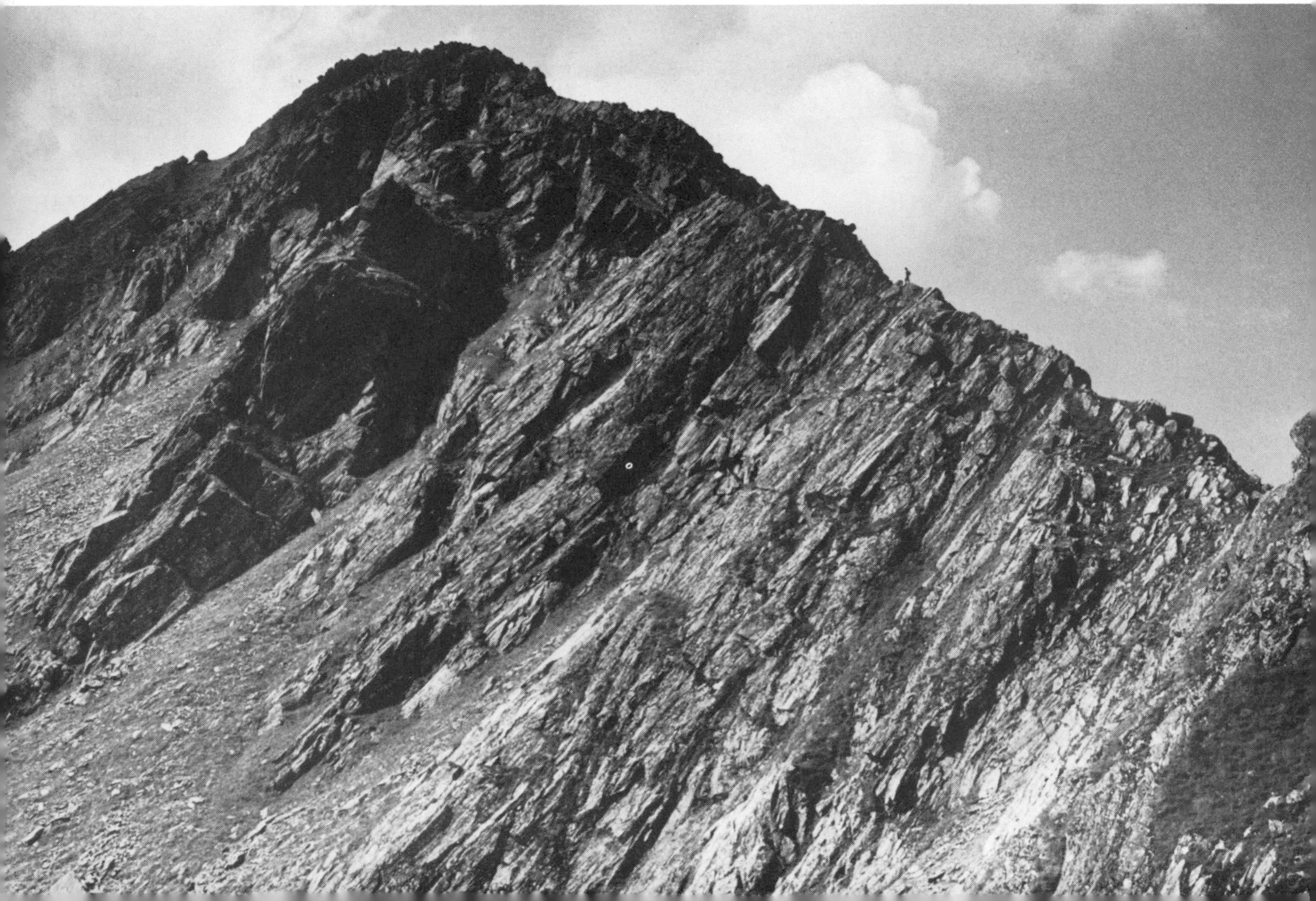

130 *A pinnacle on the Forcan Ridge*

131 *Looking towards The Saddle from Sgurr nan Forcan*

28 A'Chioch of Sgurr a' Chaorachain

The peninsula of Applecross in Wester Ross can hardly be described as a mountainous land. Much of its interior is an undulating plateau of Torridonian Sandstone, barely covered with grass and heather and dotted with little lochans which gives the impression of a desolate, almost lunar landscape. Only in the south-east does the plateau rise above seven hundred metres and it is there, facing Loch Kishorn, that one finds the three mountains of Applecross: Beinn Bhan, Sgurr a' Chaorachain and Meall Gorm.

The features which these three mountains have in common, and which are their chief glory, are the cliffs and corries of their eastern faces, where the rough summit plateaux are cut away abruptly to form terraced sandstone precipices. The eastern corrie of Sgurr a' Chaorachain is the Coire nan Arr, the giant's corrie. It is well named, for it would be easy to imagine some pre-ice-age giant building the walls and towers of this corrie with huge blocks of sandstone, which have since been weathered and eroded by thousands of years of ice, rain and wind.

The central feature of Coire nan Arr is A'Chioch, the terminal tower of Sgurr a' Chaorachain's long east ridge, which thrusts far out above the glen. The outer face of A'Chioch soars 400 metres from the floor of the corrie and is the finest sandstone buttress in the North-West Highlands.

Not surprisingly A'Chioch attracted the attention of the earliest climbers in Scotland. N. Collie, W.C. Slingsby, W. Ling and G. Glover all made ascents, but their routes on the south face were very indirect and avoided the main challenge of the buttress. J.H.B. Bell searched for a more direct way up the east face and he traversed along the ledge which girdles A'Chioch at mid-height, but he found no way of climbing upwards from the ledge. In 1952 Tom Patey and his Aberdeen companions climbed the north face of A'Chioch by a long and very hard route, but still the direct route escaped discovery. Finally in 1960 Patey returned with Chris

132 *Looking across the head of Loch Kishorn to Sgurr a' Chaorachain*

133 *A'Chioch of Sgurr a' Chaorachain*

Bonington. They traversed along the middle ledge as Bell had done several years earlier and started climbing upwards at the outermost point of the ledge, right on the nose of A'Chioch.

Patey has related how, after climbing two pitches, they found themselves belayed on a lofty balcony right on the nose of A'Chioch at its steepest point. Above them was a pronounced overhang, the rain was pouring down and the situation looked unpromising. Bonington, whose turn it was to lead, disappeared round the overhang and in a remarkably short time climbed the almost vertical wall above. What had appeared from below to be an extremely severe pitch turned out to be so well supplied with excellent holds as to be (to quote Patey) 'a glorious Difficult'. (This was a typical understatement; most climbers would agree that the pitch is a bit harder than this.) Thus the Cioch Nose route was discovered, for the steep pitch proved to be the key to the climb. In the years since the first ascent the route has become the classic climb on Torridonian Sandstone: Very Difficult in standard, perfect rock and superb exposed situations.

The ledge which encircles A'Chioch at mid-height narrows at its outer end to become one of the most sensational footpaths in Scotland, with a sheer drop below and overhanging rocks above. Just before reaching this point the Cioch Nose route

begins near a rowan sapling. The first pitch is an unsatisfactory mixture of rock and high-angle grass, but it can be improved by a variation further right. Thereafter the climb is on perfect rock with little or no vegetation. Traversing rightwards, the second pitch is an open chimney with an awkward start and an exit on the right to reach the balcony below the key pitch.

Even with the knowledge that this pitch is easier than it looks, most leaders must have a surge of adrenalin as they make the first few moves, for the exposure is considerable, the wall above is near-vertical and the holds are none too obvious from below. But holds there are, beautiful little wrinkles and notches in the rough red sandstone, and soon all feelings of fear disappear with the exhiliaration of climbing this glorious pitch, and looking down one can savour the extreme exposure. Above this wall the difficulties soon begin to diminish and the steepness relents. One continues slightly rightwards past another little rowan tree, and then directly upwards on superb rock until the top of A'Cioch is reached almost 200 metres above the start of the climb.

At this point, however, the true mountaineer will realise that he is barely half way up the east ridge of Sgurr a' Chaorachain. Ahead rises another sandstone buttress and the way is obvious, up a succession of short easy walls until a much higher wall is reached barring the front of the buttress. This wall gives another fine pitch, either at its left-hand side or directly up the centre, and above it the angle of the buttress suddenly eases. Now only scrambling remains, but it is still a long way to the summit of Sgurr a' Chaorachain, over a succession of grassy towers separated by little rocky cols. The ups and downs seem to go on for ever, but eventually the last of the cols is passed and the top of the ridge is reached.

This point turns out to be the lower of Sgurr a' Chaorachain's two summits, and it is marred by an unsightly communications aerial; it is an anti-climax to such a splendid climb. The true summit is over a kilometre distant to the south-east round the edge of the corrie, and it is worth a visit for the feeling of height and solitude which all summits should have, but which the lower top lacks. There is also a wonderful view to the south-west, across the deep glen of the Bealach nam Bo and beyond the cliffs of Meall Gorm to the distant Cuillin.

134 *The first pitch of the Cioch Nose route*
135 *The second pitch of the Cioch Nose route*

29 Fuar Tholl and the Mainreachan Buttress

The profile of Fuar Tholl (907m) seen from Lochcarron village bears, according to the local inhabitants, an uncanny resemblance to the face of the Duke of Wellington seen in profile. The Duke's nose is formed by the topmost part of the Mainreachan Buttress, but only its tip can be seen, and on the whole this aspect of the mountain is unimpressive.

From the platform of Achnashellach station, however, one gets a very different impression, for now Fuar Tholl seems to tower above the forested glen, its face lined by steep crags and gullies. From this viewpoint Mainreachan Buttress is completely hidden, and to see it one must climb high up into Coire Lair and circle round to the hidden north-west corrie of the mountain.

The walk up Coire Lair is superb. At first the path goes through the forest among rhododendron, larch and fir, with the River Lair tumbling over falls and rapids nearby. Higher up, the path emerges onto the open hillside where scattered Scots pines are the few remains of an earlier forest, and the river, now hidden in its deep ravine, is nothing but a distant murmur. In due course one arrives at the threshold of Coire Lair; ahead the glen is level and grassy for two kilometres and then the peaks close in. The path to Torridon continues towards the distant Bealach Coire Lair, below the white quartzite screes of Beinn Liath Mhor on the north side of the corrie and the contrasting dark sandstone crags of Sgor Ruadh opposite. The way to the Mainreachan Buttress, however, follows another path across the river and westwards over the shoulder of Fuar Tholl.

As one climbs round the north side of the mountain, so at last Mainreachan Buttress appears. At first one sees only its summit, but this is enough to make one pause, for its profile is steep to the point of overhanging. Soon the buttress is in full view, standing over 200 metres high at the head of the corrie in splendid isolation, the finest feature of the mountain.

136 *Fuar Tholl from Glen Carron*

137 *The north-west corrie of Fuar Tholl and the Mainreach an Buttress*

It is in every respect the archetypal Torridonian Sandstone buttress, dark and intimidating, its vertical walls streaked by black wet patches in all but the driest weather, and girdled by grass terraces. On Mainreachan Buttress, however, the terraces are few and narrow, and on the west face they disappear altogether, so that this is probably the highest and steepest sandstone wall in the Highlands.

As its appearance foretells, there are no easy routes on Mainreachan Buttress, nothing less than Severe. The original route, climbed by J.R. Marshall, W. Cole and I. Oliver in 1952, is the Enigma Route, an apt name for there was an air of the unknown about the buttress up to that year. Enigma follows the line of least resistance close to the north-east edge of the buttress, and is typical of Torridonian climbing – a succession of steep walls which often turn out to be harder than they appear from below, but there (unlike many Torridonian climbs) the rock is generally excellent.

Starting at the left hand end of the lowest terrace, the first pitch goes by a rising traverse to the right, crossing a steep crack. Traversing back left along the next terrace, one climbs a prominent groove – a strenuous pitch until a bulge at mid-height is passed. Now one is confronted by a high wall that seems to encircle the buttress. Directly ahead a huge flake stands against the wall, and from its top a splendid line of holds going right then straight up solve what promised to be a tough pitch. A short rib on the left leads to a broad terrace below the upper part of the buttress where the rock seems to be more broken, but there is still one awkward pitch before easy ground is reached. Above that the climb relents, and the only problem is one of route-finding, to find good rock and to avoid the grass.

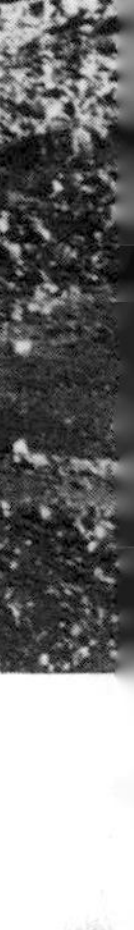

Enigma is a typically Torridonian climb, with its steep sandstone walls separated by grassy terraces along which the climber can traverse one way or the other in search of a way upwards. By contrast the three routes on the west face of the buttress, first climbed by M. Boysen and D. Alcock in 1969, are of a more formidable character altogether, for on that face there are no terraces, the rock is nearly vertical and the climbing is remarkably exposed. Typical of these climbs is Investigator, which has the reputation as one of the best climbs of its standard (Hard Severe) in the north-west. After traversing onto the face at mid-height, there is a climb of Dolomitic steepness and exposure, directly up to the top of the buttress. With routes of this character it is hardly surprising that Mainreachan Buttress shares with A'Chioch of Sgurr a' Chaorachain the reputation for the best sandstone climbing in Scotland.

138 *The north-east face of Mainreachan Buttress. Enigma Route goes directly up the edge between sunlight and shadow.*

139 *The west face of Mainreachan Buttress. Two climbers are on Investigator*

30 Beinn Eighe: the Central Buttress of Coire MhicFhearchair

The two magnificent mountains which stand side by side on the north of Glen Torridon are in marked contrast to each other. On the one hand there is Liathach with its dark terraced walls of Torridonian Sandstone, and on the other hand there is Beinn Eighe with its sweeping slopes of white quartzite.

Beinn Eighe (1010m) is the grandest quartzite mountain in Scotland, and seen from any direction the range (for it is not a single peak) presents a striking appearance: 'blanched bare and bald and white', to quote Principal Shairp. Yet there is beauty in the curving ridges which link its many peaks and the long slopes of quartzite scree which sweep down to Glen Torridon. So white is the quartzite that the mountain glistens in sunshine and gives the impression of being permanently snow-covered. This appearance is deceptive, for the smooth looking slopes turn out on closer acquaintance to be composed of unstable angular boulders which would make any ascent tedious if not actually dangerous. The climber approaching from Glen Torridon should take one of the recognised routes of ascent, such as the stalkers' path which starts near Loch Bharranch. Once on the main ridge of Beinn Eighe

140 *Beinn Eighe from Loch Coulin*

141 *Coire MhicFhearchair and the Triple Buttress*

there is a grand traverse over its seven peaks.

By contrast with the slopes above Glen Torridon, the north side of Beinn Eighe is wild, rough and precipitous; a discontinuous series of cliffs and corries making it one of the most sterile landscapes in Scotland. The finest of the corries on this side of the mountain is Coire Mhic Fhearchair, and it is in every respect one of the grandest corries in all the Scottish mountains; the classic combination of a dark lochan enclosed by towering cliffs in a truly remote setting. The feature of this corrie which gives it a unique character is the huge Triple Buttress, rising over 300 metres at the head of the corrie. The appearance of these three buttresses is enhanced by their symmetry and structure, each one being a 200 metre quartzite pillar standing on a plinth of red Torridonian Sandstone.

Whether or not one has ambitions to climb on these buttresses, Coire MhicFhearchair is well worth a visit, and once in the corrie there is an easy climb to Ruadh-stac-Mhor, the highest of Beinn Eighe's tops. The shortest route to the corrie is by the path from Glen Torridon through Coire Dubh, and round the north-west side of Sail Mhor.

The first recorded climb on the Triple Buttress was made by N. Collie and his party at the turn of the century. They climbed the gully between the Central and West buttresses until stopped near the top by an overhanging cliff, and then they traversed leftwards onto Central Buttress but had no time to

142 *Piggott's Route on the upper half of Central Buttress*

143 *Hamilton's Route on the Final Tower of Central Buttress*

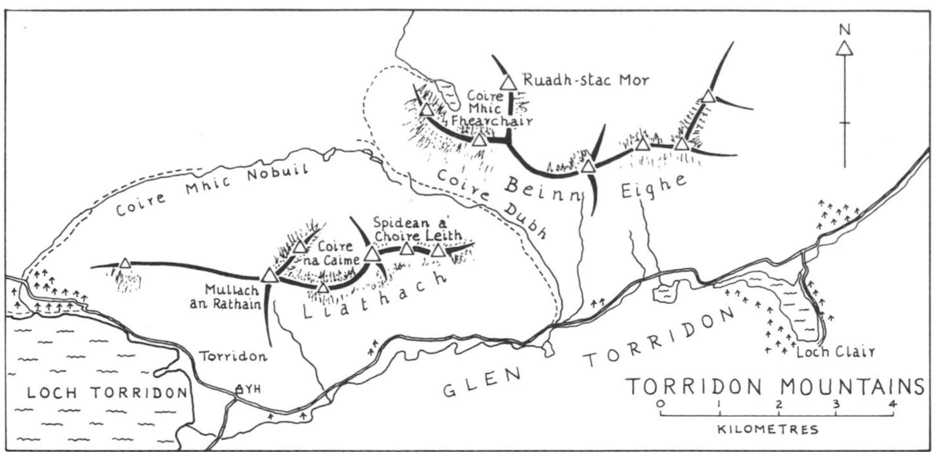

reach the top. Next day they returned to the top of the buttress and descended to the highest point they had reached the previous day. Although it was a very fine piece of exploratory mountaineering, it could hardly be described as an ascent of the Central Buttress. The first true ascent was made in 1922 by A.S. Piggott and Morley Wood, and several years later Hamish Hamilton and W. Kerr made another ascent by a completely different route.

These two routes, the former keeping close to the middle of the buttress and the latter on its right-hand side, and both of Mild Severe standard, are the usual routes on Central Buttress. It is probably true to say, however, that the buttress can be climbed by a great variety of routes, some recorded and others unrecorded, and the pleasure of climbing the Central Buttress is heightened by the absence of detailed guidebook descriptions. The climber must use his skill and judgement to find his own route, but at least he has the knowledge that routes do exist.

The sandstone plinth of the buttress has a familiar Torridonian appearance – vertical walls separated by narrow grass ledges – and in any but the driest weather the rock is likely to be streaked with dark wet patches. There are, however, lines of weakness. Piggott's route, starting near the foot of the buttress, aims to reach a dark cave about 100 metres up in the middle of the sandstone cliff. From this cave an obvious line leads up to the left by a grassy rake. An alternative on the sandstone, corresponding closely to Hamilton's route, lies much nearer West-Central Gully and follows slabs and short walls rightwards and then directly up towards the Broad Terrace. The climbing is pleasanter than Piggott's route, but less direct, and when wet the final slab is quite hard, as there is an awkward and exposed move on sloping holds right at the top.

Above Broad Terrace, Piggott's route continues directly up the quartzite buttress a few metres right of its outermost edge, but after two steep pitches the climb becomes easy, and one scrambles up to the foot of the final tower where the buttress becomes much narrower and soars up in a superb quartzite pillar. Hamilton's route on this section starts near West-Central Gully and follows steep rocks overlooking the gully, climbing upwards and rightwards in search of a breakthrough until a splendid line of holds, almost a staircase, leads back towards the crest of the buttress and the final tower.

This final tower is the finest feature of Central Buttress. Whereas the lower quartzite rocks are much fractured by horizontal and vertical cracks, the tower is more monolithic, and lines of weakness are few. About 20 metres up the front of the tower there is an obvious dark chimney; this gives a short and strenuous struggle, but it proves to be the key to the frontal ascent of the tower. A few metres to the right a large detached flake marks the start of the final section of Hamilton's route. A really fine pitch leads across the top of the flake to an exposed position at its right-hand end, followed by a steep climb up the wall above until the security of a little gully is reached.

Central Buttress ends abruptly as one pulls up over the last steep pitch and steps onto the short horizontal ridge leading to A'Choinneach Mhor. This top lives up to its name – the big mossy place – and there could hardly be a more striking contrast than that between the vertical cliffs of Coire MhicFhearchair and the horizontal expanse of green moss that covers this part of Beinn Eighe. It is a place for relaxation, giving some respite between the long climb just finished and the fast but hardly relaxing return to Glen Torridon down the quartzite screes above Coire Dubh.

31 The Traverse of Liathach

Liathach (the grey one, 1054m), is the highest of the Torridon mountains, and one of the finest in Scotland. It is a superb example of Torridonian mountain architecture, being composed of layer upon layer of reddish-grey sandstone with its summits capped by quartzite. The joints between successive layers of sandstone form horizontal terraces running across the sides of the mountain, and it is this terraced structure which is so characteristic of the Torridonian Sandstone mountains of the North-West Highlands.

Liathach is a range of several peaks extending for about five kilometres on the north side of Glen Torridon, the finest part being the two kilometre ridge between Mullach and Rathain and Spidean a' Choire Leith where the crest is narrowest and at one point splintered into a succession of pinnacles – Am Fasarinen. The south side of the mountain, especially that part below Am Fasarinen, is remarkably steep and plunges in a single sweep of 900 metres from the narrow ridge down to Glen Torridon, the terraced hillside riven by many steep and narrow gullies.

The north side of Liathach is even more impressive, though one has to walk several kilometres to reach Coire na Caime and see the innermost recesses of this wild corrie which is the heart of the mountain. There one is surrounded by a semicircle of dark buttresses and gullies dropping from the pinnacled summit ridge, but so shattered is the rock that few climbs have been done on them, and the best climbing has been done in winter when snow and ice bind the loose rock and fill the gullies.

The best mountaineering expedition on Liathach is the ascent of Mullach an Rathain by its north-east ridge (known as the Northern Pinnacles) followed by the traverse eastwards over Am Fasarinen to Spidean a' Choire Leith and beyond it to the easternmost peak, Stuc a' Choire Dhuibh Bhig. This traverse takes one round the northern side of the mountain to the head of Coire na Caime, and then along the finest sections of the ridges. In summer it is a good day's scrambling; in winter under a good cover of snow it is a magnificent day's mountaineering, much longer and more serious than the Aonach Eagach, and if conditions are hard or the weather turns bad it can easily develop into an epic.

From Coire na Caime one can reach the col at the foot of the Northern Pinnacles directly, or digress to include Meall Dearg, the northern outlier of Liathach. The Northern Pinnacles form a narrow shattered ridge with several steep steps formed by the north-east faces of successive towers. The rock is very loose, and in summer the scramble, though not difficult, requires care. In winter, if the ridge is gripped by frosty snow and ice, the ascent is more enjoyable though much more serious, and calls for some careful route-finding, usually on the right of the crest. At such times the climb has a truly Alpine ambience.

146 *Looking towards Spidean a' Choire Leith from the east end of the ridge*

Going east from Mullach an Rathain the main ridge is easy until one reaches Am Fasarinen. In summer the traverse along the crest of these pinnacles is an exhiliarating scramble, no more than Moderate in standard, but one does need a good head for heights. The pinnacles can be avoided by a narrow path lower down on the south side of the ridge; this path wends its way across gullies and round grassy buttresses to give a spectacular and exposed walk, for there is a long steep drop to Glen Torridon directly below. In winter it is probably best to keep close to the crest, for any attempt to traverse below the pinnacles on hard snow or ice may be even more difficult than climbing them directly.

Beyond Am Fasarinen the traverse becomes easy as one climbs a great pile of angular quartzite boulders to Spidean a' Choire Leith and continues along the narrow but easy ridge to Stuc a' Choire Dhuibh Bhig. The final descent to Glen Torridon needs as much care as anything, for the vertical sandstone walls which encircle the mountain can be serious obstacles to anyone making the wrong choice of route. There are, nevertheless, some fairly easy ways down to Glen Torridon, one such being the gully which starts a short distance west of Stuc a' Choire Dhuibh Bhig. However, even such relatively easy routes require care, and the traverse of Liathach ends only when the last of the sandstone terraces has been passed and easy ground is at hand.

32 The Letterewe Wilderness

The map of Wester Ross shows that north of Loch Maree there is a mountainous land stretching 25 kilometres northwards towards Little Loch Broom. It holds the lonely deer forests of Letterewe, Fisherfield and Strathnasheallag: several hundred square kilometres of mountains, lochs and moorland. In the interior of this region there are no roads and only very occasional signs of habitation; it is a land inhabited by red deer and mountain goats, visited occasionally by climbers, fishermen and stalkers.

This area has come to be regarded as the ultimate mountain wilderness in Scotland; uninhabited, unspoiled, difficult of access and ruled by landowners who have acquired the reputation for discouraging visiting climbers. This reputation is certainly justified in the stalking season, but at other times of the year the main obstacle to reaching the heart of the mountains is sheer distance. Climbers should in fact feel grateful to successive landowners who have preserved this region as a true wilderness, free of development or desecration and retaining an aura of inaccessibility. A visit to the hinterland of Letterewe or Fisherfield still has the flavour of a

147 *In the heart of the wilderness, looking from A' Mhaighdean towards Slioch*

pioneering venture into a mountain fastness, and the rewards are great for anyone who makes the effort, whether he goes to climb the crags round Carnmore or wander over remote mountain tops.

Letterewe is great country for the climber who likes to pack his tent, rope and a few days' food and just disappear into the hills. A look at the map is enough to fire the imagination; there are remote glens, some penetrated by stalkers' paths, high lochans among the mountains that promise perfect campsites, and the half dozen Munros in the heart of the area are collectively the remotest in Scotland.

Possibly the best cross-country route is from Kinlochewe to Dundonnell, although the approach from Poolewe is also attractive. The Kinlochewe to Dundonnell walk, however, has so much variety and interest that it is hard to beat; each section has its own character. There is the start from Kinlochewe along the beautifully wooded riverside to reach Loch Maree. Then suddenly the scene becomes wilder as one turns up Gleann Bianasdail; scattered pines cling to the steep hillsides and the east side of the glen is enclosed along its length by an almost continuous line of crags. At the head of the glen one comes to the desolate, windswept shore of Lochan Fada, and several trackless miles lead along its edge to reach Gleann Tulacha, which in turn leads under the crags of Beinn Lair towards the mountainous interior.

Crossing the col at the head of Gleann Tulacha, one comes to yet another sudden change in the landscape, for far below is the Fionn Loch, its head en-

148 *Looking from Martha's Peak across the Fionn Loch towards Ruadh Stac Mor and A' Mhaighdean*

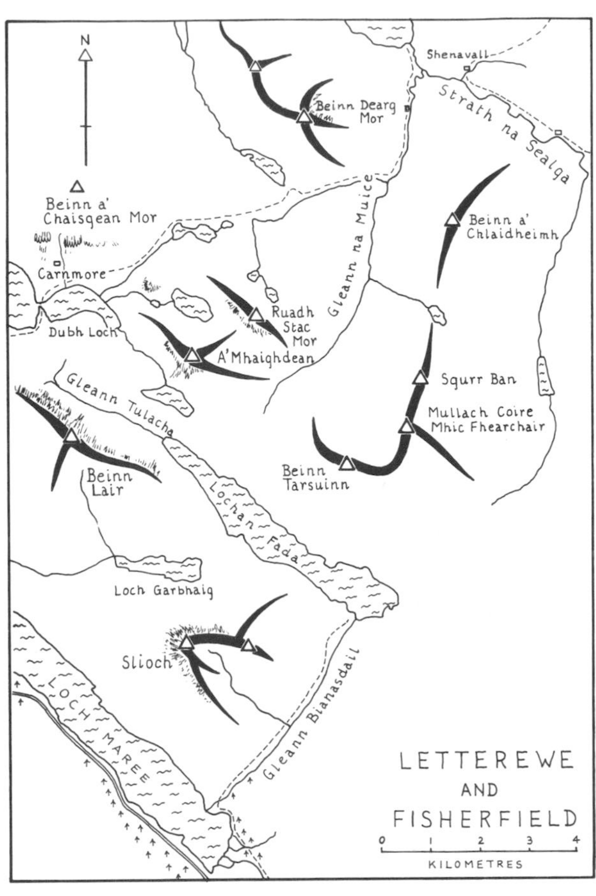

closed by crags and its lower end lost among peat moors 10 kilometres to the north-west. The Fionn Loch lives up to its name, the fair loch, for there are stretches of grass and sand round its shoreline which make delightful campsites in a glorious setting. All around are great crags: Martha's Peak on Beinn Airigh Charr, the seemingly endless cliffs of Beinn Lair and the twin cliffs, Carnmore Crag and Torr na h-Iolaire, at whose foot is the lonely house at Carnmore.

From the Fionn Loch the way north-eastwards goes either by the stalkers' path direct to Gleann na Muice, or more adventurously over some of the tops such as A'Mhaighdean (967m). This is the most inaccessible Munro in Scotland, and its superb setting among high lochans at the heart of this remote country gives it a special appeal for hill-walkers. Dedicated Munro-baggers would have no great difficulty in climbing all six Munros, starting with A'Mhaighdean or its neighbour Ruadh Stac Mor (918m), and traversing the long ridge on the east side of Gleann na Muice that ends at Beinn a' Chlaidheimh (914m).

Rather than hurrying on to Dundonnell, it is worth while stopping in beautiful Strath na Sealga, where the bothy at Shenavall is a haven for cross-country walkers and a good base from which to climb Beinn Dearg Mhor (not a Munro, but a magnificent mountain nevertheless). From Shenavall there

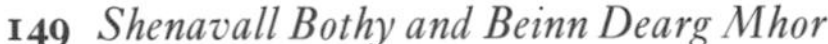

149 *Shenavall Bothy and Beinn Dearg Mhor*

remain only about three hours' walk to Dundonnell along the pleasant path which circles round the east side of An Teallach and gives glimpses of the superb peaks and corries of that mountain. Finally, the path drops down through the birch woods of Coire Chaorachain and this walk, which started in the sylvan setting of Loch Maree and crossed some of the wildest country in the Highlands, ends in the lush strath of the Dundonnell River.

The remoteness of the Letterewe mountains, and the fact that most of the great crags are hidden in the heart of the wilderness must be reasons why rock-climbers neglected these mountains for so long. By 1950 the number of climbs recorded was small: Stepped Ridge on Slioch, Martha's Peak on Beinn Airigh Charr, an indeterminate route on Torr na h-Iolaire and a very few others.Then suddenly in 1951 there was a surge of exploration; in one summer the north face of Beinn Lair, with its innumerable buttresses and gullies, was subjected to the most concerted attack that any Scottish mountain has ever suffered. A score of new routes and variations were made in the space of three months. In 1956 Mike O'Hara and his Cambridge University companions started their remarkable climbing campaigns on Carnmore Crag, Torr na h-Iolaire and other nearby crags which produced many excellent routes, including Fionn Buttress, the best of them all. In a few years Carnmore, with its combination of inaccessibility and superb climbing, became established as the most delectable goal of climbers in the north-west.

No one looking at the grassy side of Beinn Lair which faces Loch Maree would suspect that the north face is a continuous line of cliffs about five kilometres long. Admittedly many of the buttresses and gullies are very grassy and of no great interest for climbing, but there are many which are quite the opposite. The rock is a hornblende schist whose strata dips inwards, giving a profusion of small incut holds and excellent climbing – provided there is not too much grass. At the north-west end of the mountain there are several buttresses overlooking the col at the head of Gleann Tulacha which look remarkably impressive. One in particular which draws the eye is Wisdom Buttress, a narrow pillar soaring 250 metres between dark gullies. Its slabby front shows few lines of weakness and at two points seems to overhang, and its summit narrows to a slender tip.

Wisdom Buttress has all the character of a serious climb; it is steep and exposed, and in the absence of obvious lines of weakness the leader must use his own judgement in route finding. There are some fine situations, such as the tiny stance under the first overhang (fortunately well provided with belay cracks) where the second perches while his leader makes a spectacular traverse. Higher up, where the crest of the buttress overhangs again, the route goes

150 *Looking south from the shoulder of An Teallach above Shenavall*

out onto the west wall which is nearly vertical and very exposed, but the incut holds are good. Throughout the route belays are scarce and pitches long, and one gets the impression that this is not a climb on which to be caught out by rain, for the rock, good enough when dry, becomes very slippery when wet. In such conditions the standard would go up from Very Difficult to a much more serious Severe, and the possibility of having to retreat from high up on the climb due to bad weather is not a pleasant prospect.

Like all the climbs in Letterewe, Wisdom Buttress owes something of its character to the remoteness of the situation. On these routes one has the very strong feeling of climbing in the back of beyond, and this should make for added caution as well as added pleasure. In Letterewe one can sense more acutely than elsewhere the exhilaration and hazards of climbing, and appreciate that self-reliance is the paramount virtue of the mountaineer.

151 *Easy slab climbing half way up Wisdom Buttress*

152 *An exposed traverse onto the west face of Wisdom Buttress near the top of the climb*

33 The Traverse of An Teallach

Every climber's list of the great Scottish mountains is bound to include An Teallach (1062m), the magnificent range which stands above Little Loch Broom in Wester Ross. The name An Teallach means 'the forge' which fancifully, yet quite aptly, describes the appearance of the mountain when mists boil up from the corries and swirl round its many pinnacles.

An Teallach has all the characteristics of the other great Torridonian mountains further south – steep terraced walls, pinnacled ridges and deep corries. It is not a single peak, but a long branching ridge with several tops enclosing two great corries, one of which – the Toll an Lochain – is not surpassed in the north-west. One gets a grand impression of the whole mountain from the lonely Destitution Road which crosses the featureless moorland several kilometres away to the south-east.

The classic expedition on An Teallach is the traverse of all the peaks which enclose the Toll an Lochain; in this way one climbs the most interesting tops – Corrag Bhuidhe, Sgurr Fiona and Bidein a' Ghlas Thuill, the highest of them all. In summer this is an excellent scramble calling for some modest rock-climbing skill and a good head for heights, for the ridge is very narrow and exposed in places. In winter the traverse may well be a formidable undertaking, particularly if the pinnacles of Corrag Bhuidhe are plastered in snow and ice.

The mountain can be approached by way of the Garbh Allt, the stream which flows out of the Toll an Lochain. A good path starts opposite Dundonnell House and leads up through pine trees onto the open hillside where, higher up, vast pavements of glaciated sandstone make for easy walking. Eventually the Toll an Lochain is reached and it is worth going right into the corrie and resting by the side of the loch to appreciate the great cirque of peaks which encircle it. One of these peaks in particular, the Corrag Bhuidhe Buttress, rises straight

153 *The cliffs and peaks of An Teallach from Loch Toll an Lochain*

154 *On the ridge between Corrag Bhuide and Sgurr Fiona*
155 *Corrag Bhuide and Sgurr Fiona*

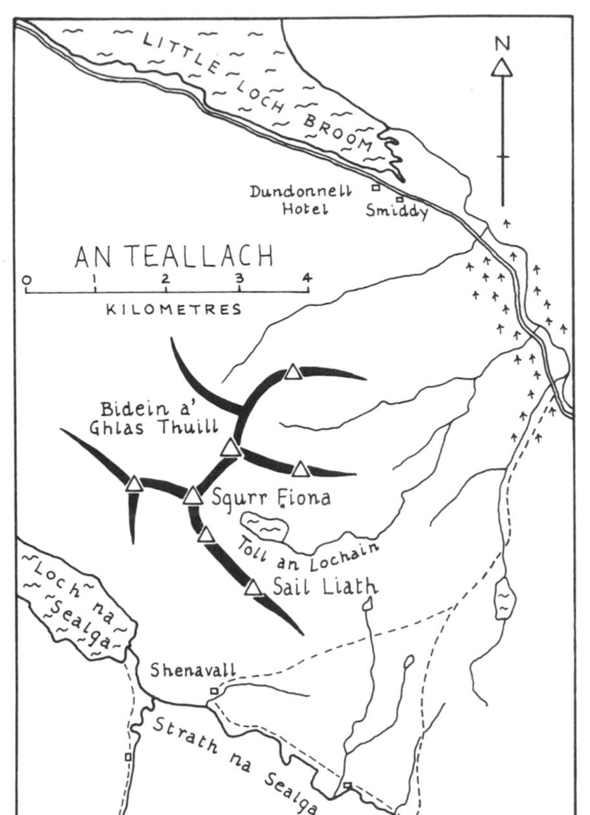

out of the dark waters of the loch.

Now to the traverse. The ridge can be easily reached from the outflow of the loch by climbing steeply westwards below the cliffs of Sail Liath to the Cadha Gobhlach, the Forked Pass. From the pass there is a short climb south-east to the quartzite capped dome of Sail Liath, the starting point for the traverse.

Returning across the Cadha Gobhlach and the peak beyond it, one soon comes to the Corrag Bhuidhe Buttress and the start of more interesting climbing. The ridge becomes steeper and narrower as it continues over the four tops of Corrag Bhuidhe, and it is possible to avoid most of the difficulties by traversing along ledges on the south-west side of the ridge. However, to enjoy the best of the scrambling on the rough red sandstone one should stay as close to the crest as possible and savour the exposure, for Loch Toll an Lochain is over five hundred metres below one's heels. Beyond Corrag Bhuidhe the ridge drops slightly to Lord Berkeley's Seat, the most sensational peak of An Teallach; on its east side there is a sheer drop for almost 100 metres into the steep slabby gully which plunges down to the corrie.

Now the ridge becomes easy again and one walks up to the beautiful pointed peak of Sgurr Fiona.

156 *On the narrow crest of Corrag Bhuide*

157 *Looking along the ridge from Sail Liath to Sgurr Fiona*

This is really the climax of the traverse, coming as it does at the end of the glorious scramble over Corrag Bhuidhe, and it is a pity that Sgurr Fiona does not have the extra height that would make it An Teallach's topmost point. To reach this there is a long descent and reascent to Bidein a' Ghlas Thuill, a peak which may appear rather featureless on the Toll an Lochain side, but one has only to take a few steps beyond the cairn to discover An Teallach's other great corrie, the Ghlas Thuill, whose precipices plunge hundreds of metres to the grassy hollow below.

On the return to Dundonnell a completely different aspect of An Teallach can be seen if one descends the north ridge from Bidein a' Ghlas Thuill and drops down into the head of Coire a' Mhuillin, where a path will be found leading down to the head of Little Loch Broom. This northern side of the mountain is a vast expanse of gravelly hillocks and grassy hollows, a complete contrast to the dark waters and pinnacled skyline of the Toll an Lochain.

34 Stac Pollaidh

North-west of Ullapool the mountain landscape of Coigach and Western Assynt is unique in Scotland. There small isolated mountains rise abruptly from an undulating plateau of Torridonian Sandstone and Lewisian Gneiss, and between them – in the hollows of the low-lying moorland – there are countless lochs and lochans, large and small. By contrast with the complex Torridonian mountains with their many peaks, ridges and corries, the little mountains of Coigach and Assynt are starkly simple – steep-sided wedges of Torridonian Sandstone. Some, capped with quartzite, have resisted erosion and their summits are rounded; others show the typical structure of sandstone peaks, and are weathered into narrow ridges and pinnacles.

The lowest of these mountains, but nevertheless one of great character, is Stac Pollaidh (613m). It rises directly above the road to Achiltibuie on the north side of Loch Lurgainn, and is one of the most accessible peaks in Scotland. In appearance it is rather like a miniature volcano; on all sides ever-steepening slopes of grass and scree sweep up to the summit, which is itself a jagged ridge of sandstone carved by wind and rain into many rounded towers

158 *Stac Pollaidh from Loch Lurgainn*

159 *On the summit ridge of Stac Pollaidh* (Photo: Anne Bennet)

160 *Looking from Stac Pollaidh towards Cul Beag*

and pinnacles. Stac Pollaidh gives the impression of being a mountain in the last stages of erosion, but for all that it has a striking appearance, as if defying the elements and the forces of nature.

It is also a mountain with a great fascination for climbers. Admittedly one can easily reach the summit ridge near its eastern end in an hour from the road, but from that point there is still some way to go to reach the summit, scrambling along the crest, up and down little towers and traversing round steep corners. The rock is superbly rough, scoured clean by Atlantic storms, and the scramble is delightful. On the south side of the summit ridge there are pinnacles and narrow subsidiary ridges with any number of short climbs on them, some very hard. Even hill-walkers intent on reaching the topmost point will have to do a little bit of rock-climbing to surmount or circumvent the small tower just east of the summit.

The best rock-climbing on Stac Pollaidh is on the fine sandstone buttress, over 100 metres high, which forms its western bastion. As elsewhere on the mountain the rock is rough and clean, weathered into many ledges and cracks. On the south side of the buttress, directly below the summit, there are hard climbs up the prominent twin grooves and on the steep wall just to the right of these. More in keeping, however, with the carefree nature of Stac Pollaidh climbing is the West Buttress, the seaward ridge of the mountain. There is a little pinnacle, the Forefinger, at the foot of the cliff and this is a landmark from which to start. Above it one climbs by walls, slabs and cracks, choosing one's own route almost anywhere, for the buttress is well broken up and many variations of about Difficult standard are possible.

There are some features, however, which all routes on the West Buttress have in common; these are the rough red sandstone, the exhilarating exposure high up on the prow of the mountain and the limitless view across the white sands of Achnahaird to the waters of the Minch and distant Lewis.

35 The Pinnacle Ridge of Sgurr nan Gillean

Mountaineering in Skye may be said to have had its birth in 1836, for it was in that year that Professor William Forbes (guided by a local forester, Duncan MacIntyre) reached the summit of Sgurr nan Gillean (the peak of the young men, 965m), the first of the Cuillin mountains to be climbed. Their route, round the east side of the mountain and up the south-east ridge, was a remarkable achievement, even though it is now regarded as the 'tourist route'. Other climbers were slow to follow in the professor's footsteps, and thirty years or more elapsed before the Visitor's Book at Sligachan Inn began to record increasingly frequent ascents of the peak.

In those years Sligachan Inn was mecca for mountaineers going to Skye, all of whom climbed (or at least attempted to climb) Sgurr nan Gillean, for it was the nearest of the Cuillins and one of the few which (before the arrival of Alexander Nicolson and the Pilkington brothers) had been climbed. Sligachan retained its place at the centre of Cuillin climbing for many years; Norman Collie, possibly the greatest of the pioneer climbers, returned there again and again until his death, and John Mackenzie, undoubtedly the greatest and most respected of

161 *Sgurr nan Gillean and the Pinnacle Ridge*

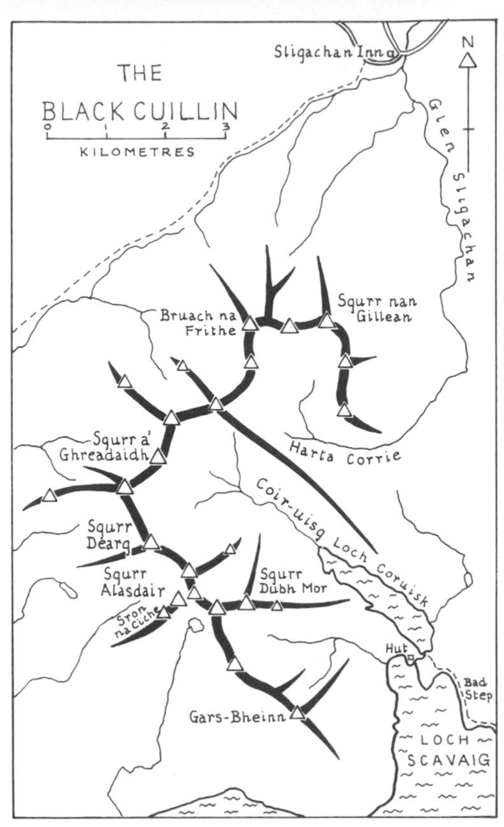

Cuillin guides, lived a few miles away at Sconser. Gradually however the centre of Cuillin climbing shifted to Glen Brittle, which had the advantage of being closer to the highest peaks and the great cliffs of Coire Lagan.

The arrival of Charles and Lawrence Pilkington at Sligachan in 1880 heralded an era of first ascents and new routes. That year they climbed Sgurr nan Gillean by the west and north ridges. The north ridge, which falls from the summit of the mountain directly towards Sligachan, is better known as the Pinnacle Ridge, but from Sligachan its real character is not apparent. Only when one sees the ridge in profile, from the east or west, does it reveal itself as a succession of pinnacles; the first two are mere steps in the ridge, the next two are well-defined and sharply pointed towers, and the final pinnacle is the summit of Sgurr nan Gillean itself. No other Scottish mountain has a more elegant ridge.

The ascent of Sgurr nan Gillean by the Pinnacle Ridge and the descent by the West Ridge is one of the finest traverses in the Cuillins. Its standard is Difficult, so that by modern reckoning it is little more than a scramble, but the character and situation of the route are so superb, and the climbing so

162 *Knight's Peak* (left) *and the summit of Sgurr nan Gillean*

163 *On the west ridge of Sgurr nan Gillean*

164 *Evening in the Cuillin. Sgurr nan Gillean and Marsco from Clach Glas*

enjoyable that the grading seems irrelevant.

The approach to the foot of the Pinnacle Ridge brings one below the west face of the first pinnacle, and there is good scrambling on rough gabbro for about 100 metres up this face to reach the crest of the ridge. The next section is an easy scramble over the second to the top of the third pinnacle. There suddenly the character of the climb becomes more serious; the south side of the pinnacle drops steeply and the situation is exposed. One descends a few metres onto a narrow ridge and then down the steep wall on its west side (possibly by abseil) to reach a little gully which leads easily to the col. This is the most awkward part of the ridge, and the ascent to the fourth pinnacle, though quite steep, is straightforward.

The fourth pinnacle is also known as Knight's Peak after Professor Knight who made the first ascent in 1873 as a variation to the original route. His companion, a local guide named Macpherson, was so overawed by the difficulty and danger of the climb that he vowed he would never go up that mountain again, but like most climbers who make such vows, he changed his mind. Few present-day climbers have any difficulty in traversing this pinnacle and scrambling up to the summit of Sgurr nan Gillean, but this is not surprising. A hundred years have brought great changes in climbers' views of the mountains, and peaks which once inspired awe and fear are now climbed with hardly a thought of danger.

The descent of the West Ridge starts without much difficulty, but the ridge becomes narrower as it drops towards the col. This upper part was first descended by Nicolson in 1865, but he quit the crest in favour of a narrow gully, Nicolson's Chimney, by which he reached the screes at the foot of the ridge. The best part comes lower down; at one point the crest of the ridge is only a few feet wide, exposed, and barred by a little pinnacle, the famous Gendarme, and one must either sidle round it or descend a steep little chimney on the north side. Below the Gendarme the ridge becomes easy and one strolls down to the Bealach a' Bhasteir.

From this col there is an easy descent into Coire a' Bhasteir and so back to Sligachan. Alternatively, one can continue the traverse over Am Basteir and the Basteir Tooth, but this involves some quite difficult climbing on the west face of the Tooth if a direct descent is made. In fact these two peaks are best traversed in the opposite direction, from west to east, and if this is combined with the traverse of Sgurr nan Gillean, descending by the Pinnacle Ridge, it makes a great day's climbing.

36 Eastern Buttress and the Coire Lagan Traverse

At about the turn of the century climbers began to forsake Sligachan Inn, which was becoming overrun by tourists, in favour of remote Glen Brittle, where they found shelter and hospitality at Glenbrittle House and Mary Campbell's cottage. One event at that time which, more than any other, stimulated rock-climbing on the Glen Brittle side of the Cuillins was Norman Collie's discovery in 1899 of the Cioch,

165 *The Cioch*

166 *Climbers on Sron na Ciche, the first pitch of Integrity* 167 *Perfect gabbro on the Eastern Buttress*

the blunt little pinnacle projecting from the centre of the great cliff-face of Sron na Ciche. Descending Coire Lagan late one summer evening, he saw a shadow cast across a smooth slab high up on the face, and realised that it could only be caused by a huge rock projecting from the cliff. In 1906 he returned with the guide John Mackenzie, climbed up the edge of the slab and reached the top of the rock which on the inspiration of Mackenzie was christened A'Chioch, or more commonly the Cioch.

From that time Glen Brittle became the home of Cuillin climbing, and Sron na Ciche the mecca of rock-climbers in Skye. Two of the most dedicated climbers in the following years were Guy Barlow and E.W. Steeple. Barlow, not knowing of Collie's ascent of the Cioch, climbed it a month later with H.B. Buckle by a different route, and these two deserve credit for their independent discovery, for Collie, ever aloof and reserved, had told few climbers in Glen Brittle of his own achievement. Barlow and Steeple went on to explore the Cuillins nearly every summer for many years, braving midges and rain to camp in the high corries, and no other partnership has produced more new climbs in Skye.

Their best discovery on Sron na Ciche was Eastern Buttress Direct, a climb with the reputation of being one of the most delightful in Skye. For 200 metres it follows the crest of the buttress facing the Cioch across Eastern Gully; a succession of exhilarating pitches lead up from ledge to ledge, the rock is gabbro at its best, rough and reliable, and the climbing is supremely enjoyable.

168 *Looking down the last pitch of Eastern Buttress to the Cioch, and beyond to Loch Brittle*

169 *Looking from Sgurr Alasdair northwards towards Sgurr nan Gillean*

Memorable among the many pitches is a short narrow chimney where stout climbers may have a bit of a struggle to surmount the final chockstone, while thin climbers may possibly find it easier to climb up the interior of the chimney and exit through a hole in its roof. Immediately above there is another excellent pitch which starts with an exposed step from the tip of a little pinnacle onto a smooth slab, and continues up a shallow groove by thin fingery cracks. By common consent the crux is the Very Difficult wall split by a thin crack at the top of the buttress. In past years the small holds became polished by the passage of nailed boots, and they might have disappeared altogether had not Vibram-soled boots replaced nails. Nowadays the reputation of this pitch is rather diminished, for not only do modern boots make it easier, but modern methods of protection enable the leader to fix running belays in the crack whenever he feels in need of psychological support.

Eastern Buttress ends with a scramble up to the broad bouldery shoulder of Sron na Ciche, but the day's climbing does not end there. One of the great pleasures of Cuillin climbing is to combine rock-climbing with a traverse over two or three peaks of the main ridge, and there is no better sequel to a climb on Sron na Ciche than the traverse of the peaks encircling Coire Lagan. Days such as this are the essence of Cuillin climbing, and the Coire Lagan traverse is the best section of the main ridge.

The first point of interest is the Bad Step, a steep pitch on the ascent to Sgurr Alasdair (993m) from Sgurr Sgumain (947m). The rock is basalt, smooth and slippery if wet, and the pitch seems to overhang slightly for a few metres; certainly one feels rather out of balance as one moves up. There is, however, an easier alternative route a short distance to the south.

Sgurr Alasdair is a splendid peak, worthy of being the highest of the Cuillins, and from its sharp summit there is a glorious view of the whole twisting chain of peaks from Gars Bheinn to distant Gillean. Nearer at hand the steep sides of the mountain plunge down to deep corries and emerald lochans far below.

The traverse continues along the narrow ridge of Sgurr Thearlaich (984m), and some care is needed descending to the Bealach Mhic Coinnich. Beyond this col Sgurr Mhic Coinnich (948m) rears up steeply and the classic, but not the easiest, route is King's Chimney. This steep corner, topped by an overhang, looks formidable, but so good are the holds that the climb turns out to be much easier than appears likely from below.

There follows a long easy descent to the next col, the Bealach Coire Lagan, and from there the ascent to the next top, An Stac, is a long scramble up a ridge which is steep and rather loose, though only Moderate in standard. From An Stac one looks up at the narrow edge of the Inaccessible Pinnacle (986m), a huge flake of gabbro which has resisted weathering better than its neighbouring rocks and now forms Scotland's sharpest summit. The first ascent was made by the Pilkington brothers in 1880 by the east ridge – the edge of the Pinnacle which rises above An Stac. This ridge is easy-angled and no more than a Moderate scramble, but one needs a good head for heights, for the ridge is very narrow and the exposure considerable as one nears the top. In the days of the first ascent, however, it must have been a nerve-wracking climb, for the crest of the ridge was composed of loose boulders which have now been trundled down to make things a bit safer.

The Inaccessible Pinnacle is the only one of the Munros reserved for rock-climbers, and it is a fitting climax to the Coire Lagan traverse. On its airy summit, as on all true pinnacles, one may well wonder how to get down. By contrast with the east ridge, the west end of the Pinnacle is short and steep; however, with the rope round a suitable belay there is no difficulty in reaching *terra firma* a short distance from the cairn of Sgurr Dearg. From there the return to Glen Brittle towards the setting sun is a mere walk down the west ridge.

37 Coir' Uisg and the Dubhs Ridge

Coir' Uisg, meaning the corrie of water, is at the heart of the Cuillin mountains, enclosed on three sides by their steep peaks and ridges, and holding in its depths Loch Coruisk, the grandest of all Scottish mountain lochs.

Painters and writers, who were amongst the earliest visitors to Coir' Uisg, gave it a reputation as a gloomy and forbidding place, whose dark loch was overshadowed by beetling crags. But this is far from the truth. When the sun shines, the waters of Loch Coruisk sparkle and the corrie is filled with brightness. Only when grey clouds gather over the peaks and rain-torrents cascade down the mountainsides does Coir' Uisg live up to its name and its reputation.

The great pleasure of being at Loch Coruisk, for mountaineers at least, is the feeling of solitude and isolation, of being in a sanctuary at the very heart of the Cuillins and able to enter fully into the spirit of these hills. There is a feeling of inaccessibility, but this is imagined rather than real for one can sail from Mallaig or Elgol to Loch Scavaig and reach Loch Coruisk with hardly any effort. Access on foot is more strenuous. The shortest approach is from Kilmarie in Strathaird, eight kilometres away, but

170 *Evening at Loch Coruisk*

this route involves crossing the Bad Step, a narrow ledge across a slab overlooking Loch Scavaig. The reputation of this *mauvais pas* is worse than its reality, but it has helped to preserve the remote and unspoiled character of Coir'Uisg.

Climbs on the Coir'Uisg side of the Cuillins have the same character. They are long, remote and rarely-visited, having the atmosphere of real mountaineering. The most popular of these climbs, albeit one of the easiest, is the Dubhs Ridge, the easy-angled, slabby ridge which rises from the edge of Loch Coruisk for over 600 metres to Sgurr Dubh Beag (732m), and continues to Sgurr Dubh Mor (944m) and Sgurr Dubh na Da Bheinn (938m). This is a grand route for making the traverse from Coir'Uisg to Glen Brittle, far better than the trudge up any of the boulder-strewn corries and cols which offer alternative ways.

Climbing the Dubhs Ridge is hardly a rock-climb in the usually accepted sense; rather it is a carefree scramble, sometimes just a walk, up hundreds of metres of rough gabbro slabs set at an easy angle. One can wander wherever the spirit moves, choosing an easy line or searching for difficulties to test oneself, for there are places where the slabs are steep and holdless enough to make one think. The spirit of the climb is well evoked by two verses commemorating the deeds of two early presidents of the Scottish Mountaineering Club:

Said Maylard to Solly one day in Glen Brittle,
All serious climbing, I vote, is a bore;
Just for once, I Dubh Beag, you'll agree to do little,
And as less we can't do, let's go straight to Dubh Mor.

So now when they seek but a day's relaxation,
With no thought in the world but of viewing the views,
And regarding the mountains in mute adoration,
They call it not 'climbing', but 'doing the Dubhs'.

171 *Looking across Loch Scavaig to the Cuillin*

172 *Scrambling up the Dubhs Ridge*

Beyond the summit of Sgurr Dubh Beag the ridge drops steeply, and a few metres down on the west side of the peak one will likely find some old slings to show that most climbers abseil down the steep pitch below. From the col, the ridge continues, no longer slabby but typical of the rest of the Cuillins – narrow and broken – over Sgurr Dubh Mor to Sgurr Dubh na Da Bheinn on the Main Ridge. If one is traversing to Glen Brittle, the finest continuation is along the Main Ridge to Sgurr Thearlaich and Sgurr Alasdair, crossing the notorious Thearlaich-Dubh gap, whose difficulties are greater than anything on the Dubhs Ridge. On the other hand, if the day is hot the temptation will be strong to drop down to either Coir a' Ghrunnda or Coir' an Lochain to swim in the cool green waters of their lochans.

173 *On the ridge to Sgurr Dubh Mor*

174 *Climbing out of the Thearlaich-Dubh Gap*

38 The Traverse of Clach Glas and Blaven

Blaven (or Bla Bheinn, 928m) is the highest of a small group of the Black Cuillin which stands in the Strathaird peninsula a few miles east of the main Cuillin Ridge. Three peaks form a high and isolated ridge, the jagged spine of Strathaird: Blaven at the south end, Clach Glas (790m) in the middle and Garbh-Bheinn (806m) at the north end.

Although quite separate from the main Cuillin Ridge, Blaven and Clach Glas have the same features – steep sides, narrow ridges and the rough gabbro rock that delights the climber. However, being apart from the rest of the Cuillin, they have an added character all of their own, their height apparently magnified by their splendid isolation, and it is little wonder that many people consider Blaven to be the finest mountain in Skye. Certainly, as one comes along the road from Broadford to Torrin, the sudden appearance of Blaven and Clach Glas rising above Loch Slapin and the crofts of Torrin is one of the great sights of Skye, whether the peaks are clear or have wreaths of misty rain trailing across their ridges.

The traverse of Clach Glas and Blaven is the classic expedition on these hills; there is grand scrambling along the ridge and, on a clear day, wonderful views on all sides. The traverse is probably best done from north to south, and Garbh-Bheinn can easily be included. The usual starting point is at the head of Loch Slapin, the approach from Sligachan being much longer.

Two kilometres up the Allt na Dunaiche one should follow its northern tributary to reach the col north of Clach Glas. A finer but much longer approach to this col can be made by climbing Sgurr nan Each, and scrambling along its rocky crest to reach the ridge half a kilometre south-east of Garbh-Bheinn, which can also be climbed before returning to the col below Clach Glas.

From this point Clach Glas looks a most impressive little peak, its summit steep on all sides. How-

175 *Clach Glas and Blaven from the north-west*

176 *In this view from Garbh-Bheinn mighty Blaven dwarfs the peak of Clach Glas*

177 *Looking up the north ridge of Clach Glas*

178 *Descending southwards from the summit of Clach Glas*

ever, appearances can be deceptive, and the first part of the ridge is quite easy scrambling as far as the little pinnacle which is such a prominent feature of the hill as seen from Loch Slapin. The last 50 metres is much steeper; one can climb directly up the ridge or more easily by a little gully a few metres down on the west side followed by a delightful pitch, steep and exposed, but with abundant holds, leading to the summit.

The ridge leading down to the Clach Glas-Blaven col is narrow, and drops steeply in places. Looking back at the topmost part of the ridge just below the summit, one can understand why the early climbers were so impressed by this apparently knife-edged tower which turns out to be something of an imposter. The descent presents no problems if one remembers when in doubt to keep on the east side of the ridge, and soon the col is reached and a little grassy hollow makes a perfect resting place.

The climb to the summit of Blaven is quite different from the narrow Clach Glas ridge, for one is now on the dark north face of the mountain, and in misty weather there may be some confusion in this maze of scree ledges, steep walls and narrow gullies. The path goes leftwards at first to give a glimpse of the Prow and the Horn, two impressive features of Blaven's north-east corrie. Then one traverses back to the right and works upwards by a short wall and a scree-filled gully to reach the foot of another little gully filled with chockstones. This gives a good scramble, and from the top of this gully one quickly reaches easy ground and the cairns which mark the tourist route on its way from the Allt na Dunaiche up Coire Uaigneich to the summit of Blaven.

On a clear day this summit is one of the great viewpoints in Scotland. The eye can range along the whole length of the Cuillin Ridge, counting every peak, then southwards across the sea to Rum and Eigg, round to the mainland mountains of Knoydart and Kintail and north to the graceful curves of the Red Cuillin. The whole landscape of Skye and the western seaboard is at one's feet.

39 The Trotternish High Level Walk

Although Skye is always associated in climbers' minds with the Black Cuillin, one should not forget that there are other hills on the island which are well worth attention. This is certainly true at those times (which occur all too often) when the Black Cuillin are shrouded in mist and rain while other parts of the island are enjoying better weather, possibly even sunshine.

To the east of the main Cuillin peaks are the Red Hills above Broadford and the hills of Lord Macdonald's Forest above Sligachan, sometimes called the Red Cuillin. These hills are well named, for they are composed of red granite which has weathered to give rounded contours and scree-covered slopes; it is this scree which is their most obvious feature, and probably deters many hill-walkers from climbing them. This is unfortunate, for these are fine little hills with a character of their own, and there are some good walks along the tops such as the traverse from Marsco to Glamaig.

Quite different in character are the hills of Trotternish, the northernmost district of Skye. There a long escarpment extends for thirty kilometres from just north of Portree almost to the northern tip of Trotternish. Although the highest point of this long ridge, The Storr, is only 718m, and most

179 *Looking north from Blaven towards Marsco, the Red Cuillin and Garbh-Bheinn*

180 *The Old Man of Storr*

of the other tops are about 600 metres high, these hills are worth a visit not only to walk along their crest, but also to explore the spectacular pinnacles and rock architecture at The Storr and the Quiraing.

The Storr is easily climbed from the road just north of Loch Leathan. On the east side of the hill there is a beautiful grassy corrie backed by the huge unclimbed cliffs of The Storr itself, and round the outer rim of the corrie is a fantastic line of pinnacles dominated by the Old Man of Storr. The whole scene of corrie, cliffs and pinnacles is reminiscent of some ancient temple or stone circle, and it would not be difficult to imagine worshippers of the sun or moon gathering in this strange natural amphitheatre. The Old Man of Storr is a 50 metre pillar of weathered basalt, overhanging round its base and tapering to a slender tip. It has been climbed by two distinct routes, but they are both Very Severe; the rock is loose and so the Old Man has remained something to be admired rather than climbed.

From the summit of The Storr there is the prospect of a grand walk northwards along the spine of Trotternish. All along the crest of the ridge the turf is soft and springy, making walking a pleasure, especially after the rough unyielding gabbro of the Cuillin. On the east side of the ridge there is an almost continuous escarpment, a line of basalt cliffs along whose edge this delightful hill-walk unfolds itself over a succession of tops which resemble the headlands of some high sea-cliff thrusting out to the east. On both sides, far below, the crofting lands of Trotternish are spread out, with dozens of white cottages dotting the low-lying moors, and beyond the Sound of Raasay rise the Torridon mountains.

One can wander northwards from The Storr for as far as the spirit moves; it is always easy to descend westwards across the moors towards Loch Snizort, and at several of the cols it is possible to drop down into the green corries on the east side of the ridge.

Far to the north the spine of Trotternish ends at Meall na Suiramach, a flat-topped hill whose eastern edge holds the most spectacular corner of Skye's mountain scenery – the Quiraing. Huge landslips have left a maze of pinnacles, fissured crags and narrow gullies below the cliff which encircles this side of the hill. The Needle is a slender spire guarding the southern entrance to an inner amphitheatre, which is even stranger than the one at The Storr. At its centre there is a raised grassy plateau called the Table, which is almost as smooth and flat as a bowling green. The name Quiraing is derived from Cuith Raing, meaning the pillared stronghold, and one certainly has the feeling of being in a natural castle. Its eastern perimeter is a line of crags and towers forming a high wall, with narrow gaps through which there are fascinating glimpses of the sea far below and the mainland mountains beyond.

181 *The ramparts of the Quiraing*

40 The Cuillin of Rum

The Parish of the Small Isles consists of four islands lying in the Sea of the Hebrides; they are the islands of the unforgettable names – Rum, Eigg, Muck and Canna. Of the four, Rum alone is mountainous; the highest of its mountains, grouped in the south-east corner of the island, are called the Cuillin of Rum. By comparison with their famous neighbours the Cuillin of Skye, the Rum peaks are certainly lower, less numerous and less starkly jagged and precipitous. Yet they lack nothing in character and variety; each peak, being quite separate from its neighbours, has its own personality, and they are given added distinction by their Norse names. There is, too, a sense of adventure about going to Rum; gone are the days when the island was virtually forbidden territory, but still (thanks to the policy of the Nature Conservancy) it keeps its aura of inaccessibility.

Five peaks over seven hundred metres and three lower tops make up the Cuillin of Rum. The traverse of these peaks is one of the best day's ridge-walking and scrambling in Scotland; it is full of interest and variety without being unduly strenuous or difficult, and it is not to be compared with the Skye Cuillin traverse either for length or difficulty. Nevertheless,

182 *The Island of Rum from the sands at Arisaig*

like the Skye ridge, it gives the same feeling of treading a narrow mountain highway between sea and sky.

The mail-boat calls at Loch Scresort on the east side of Rum, and there are good camp-sites on the lochside near the pier. The approach to the mountains starts only a few hundred metres away, following a path through the woods behind Kinloch Castle. This path leads for a couple of kilometres up the rather featureless Coire Dubh, and brings one to the bealach between Barkeval (591m) and Hallival (723m) from where Barkeval can be quickly climbed before continuing on one's way to Hallival. A much more attractive approach to Hallival can be made by taking the path which goes south from Loch Scresort round the east side of the island. After two and a half kilometres one can follow the stream up into Coire nan Grunnd, the most beautiful of the high mountain corries in Rum. From there a steep climb up the north-east skyline of Hallival (avoiding various minor crags) leads to the summit.

From Hallival the ridge drops southwards in a series of short rock steps towards Askival (812m), the highest of the Rum peaks. The ascent of Askival from the col is the best part of the traverse. A narrow grassy ridge leads to a rock tower, the Askival Pinnacle, whose steep front bars the way ahead. Although it is possible to avoid the Pinnacle by a narrow track on the east side of the ridge, it is far better to climb it directly by cracks and ledges on its west face, barely Difficult in standard. Beyond the Pinnacle the ridge continues to give delightful

183 *Hallival from Coire nan Grunnd*

scrambling along its narrow crest to the summit, a wonderful viewpoint from which one can survey all Rum and the seas beyond.

The traverse continues with a steep descent due west to the grassy col called the Bealach an Oir, followed by a more gradual climb to the sharp twin tops of Trallval (702m). An interesting feature of these highest peaks of Rum are the many little burrows in the hillsides and on grassy ledges. These are the nesting places of the Manx shearwater, a strange bird of the ocean which digs a little burrow for its nest and lays a single egg early in summer. In the daytime the birds are at sea in search of food, which explains why they are not seen; but at night they return to land to feed their young and anyone on these hills after dark will hear the night air full of the whirring of their wings as they fly to and from their burrows.

From Trallval the last part of the ridge goes south. The descent to the Bealach and Fhuarain is steep and stony, but there is a faint track which should be carefully followed in misty weather as there are cliffs a short distance west. From the bealach, Ainshval (781m) rises steeply, and the lowest rocky buttress on its north ridge can be easily circumvented to the

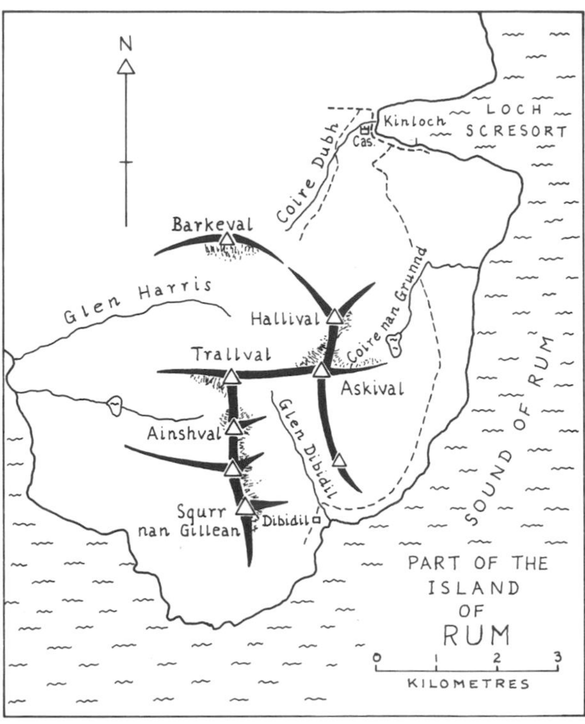

184 *Looking north from Askival towards Hallival and the cloud-capped Cuillin of Skye*

185 *The Askival Pinnacle* (Photo: Arthur Bennet)

186 *Looking east from the summit of Trallval across the Sound of Rum towards the mainland*

187 *Sgurr nan Gillean and Ainshval from the north*

west. Higher up, the ridge is rather smooth and slippery in wet weather, and in these conditions, or in a high wind, a traverse just below the crest on the east side may be preferred. At the top of this rise the summit of Ainshval is suddenly reached, and the character of the ridge changes again, becoming broad and grassy as one continues over a small top to the final peak, Sgurr nan Gillean (764m). It is this continuously changing character from peak to peak which is one of the charms of the Rum ridge.

At Sgurr nan Gillean the last problem of the day may well be how to return to one's base at Loch Scresort, only seven kilometres away as the eagle soars over Glen Dibidil, but for the climber the way must be less direct. There are two possibilities. One is to descend to Dibidil cottage at the foot of Glen Dibidil and return along the path which goes round the east side of the island; but this path is by no means level, and climbs over 200 metres on its way back to Loch Scresort. The alternative is to retrace one's steps along the ridge as far as the Bealach an Fhuarain, then contour round the south-east side of Trallval to the Bealach an Oir and continue contouring across the corrie on the west side of Askival to the bealach at the head of Coire Dubh. This route is probably quicker, and has the advantage on a fine summer day of prolonging this grand mountain walk. One can pause at the head of Coire Dubh until the sun has dropped below the Western Isles and the summit rocks of Askival turn red in the evening glow, and then stroll down the corrie to a welcoming camp fire on the shore of Loch Scresort.

Index

I Mountains

II Climbs

III Climbers